The Education of Children

By Alfred Adler

Introduction by
Rudolph Dreikurs, M.D.

Translated by
Eleanore and Friedrich Jensen, M.D.

Gateway Editions, Ltd.
South Bend, Indiana

Manufactured in the United States of America, 6–78

Library of Congress Catalog Card Number: 75-126155

International Standard Book Number: 0-89526-981-3

CONTENTS

INTRODUCTION

READING this book, one is impressed with the fact that what Adler knew and proposed, over forty years ago, is equally valid today, though still hardly known by educators, parents and teachers. He was so far ahead of his time.

Adler showed how one can understand children who are deviant, maladjusted or deficient when one perceives their goal and knows their private logic. Without such knowledge, most corrective efforts miss their mark and often lead to increased deficiencies rather than to improvement.

Adler described some fundamental rules for raising children. Of crucial importance is the development of the child's social interest. Social feeling is the barometer of the child's normalcy, he stated. On this principle Adler built his pedagogical technique. When the child begins to fail in school, he has begun to lose faith in himself, and seeks the path of quickest psychological success, from his point of view, striving for significance and supremacy, even through useless means. Adler recognized that no education is possible except for children "who look hopefully and joyfully on the future."

Adler had the courage to state that no child should be considered hopeless. But no one can exert a beneficial influence on the child who does not recognize his strength and abilities, even though he may outwardly fail. There are so many ways in which adults show their lack of confidence in the child, thereby undermining his feeling of belonging and preventing his adjustment. The factors that Adler considered harmful are still evident today: the effects of bad anticipation, for example, the aftermath of bad report cards, the competitive classroom where few excel at the expense of many.

While Adler contributed greatly in helping parents to deal effectively with the child, he recognized the school as the decisive factor in bringing up a new generation. His emphasis on the potential of the school is in direct contrast to present practices. We do not admit the failure of our teachers and of our schools to teach every child to read and write, and the increasing number of children who do not learn these fundamental skills are no longer considered the victims of an inadequate educational system, but of forces beyond the teacher's province. First, the teacher blames the parents; then, the bad influence of the environment. "Cultural deprivation" is now another reason for the teacher's inability. There is the constant flow of "scientific research," which gives teachers an alibi. It is either the low I.Q. or the slow development of boys or—more recently—dyslexia, minimal brain damage, cerebral dysfunction, perceptual deficiency that are supposedly responsible for the educational failure of children. Adler recognized the fallacy of the I.Q. test; in his time, all the other excuses for poor teaching results had not yet been "discovered."

Adler assumed—and his students, primarily Spiel in Vienna, the organizer of the Adlerian Experimental School, proved—that the school, when properly administered, can make up for the deficiencies in the early rearing of children. "The ideal school should be a place, not merely for book knowledge, but a place in which the knowledge and the art of living should be taught." We know today that the teacher

vi

is in a position, primarily because of her ability to work with the group and thereby to affect the concepts and values of her students, to undo all the harm that the family and the community have done to the child.

Adler realized that we cannot wait for the ideal school to overcome the deficiencies of early upbringing. How far should school and home be responsible for influencing children? Adler made a classic statement in this regard. "The hope of preparing the children of tomorrow rests primarily on converting the schools and teachers—although the cooperation of the parents is, of course, never rejected." While the teacher should welcome and stimulate the cooperation of the parents, she does not have to depend on it.

Our present practices limit the cooperation of parents. They are blamed for the child's deficiencies, accused of negligence and hostility and made to feel guilty, like criminals almost. It is a common practice for teachers to send "love letters" to the parents when the child fails or disturbs. Why do they send these notes? They usually say that the parents want to know. Does the teacher always do what the parents want? Of course not. The next excuse is that the parents "ought to know." Why? If the parents have exerted a good influence on the child, he probably will not be in trouble. And does the teacher really expect that the parents *can* do something to correct the child's deficiencies and misbehavior? Upon careful exploration it usually becomes obvious why teachers send such notes. They feel so defeated by the child in their classrooms that they want to "mess it up" for him at home. And in this, they succeed.

In line with Adler's concern with the school, his first psychological training of educators took place in a school, presenting cases to the whole staff. Later, he transferred his corrective group approaches to the community and established guidance centers, where the teacher could also participate, for parents. He realized that if parents fail to influence the child properly, the parents need education, not therapy. Well-informed teachers can help the parents. Teachers receive professional training and can acquire methods that are effective in a democratic setting, while parents have to rely on tradition, which no longer is an adequate guide.

Adler concludes this book with five case histories. These examples are not only highly instructive; their deeper significance lies in the fact that Adler presented here a technique that is very effective in training the psychological sensitivity of parents and teachers. He took every statement made and tried to interpret its meaning. In doing so he introduced guessing as a scientifically valid form of investigation. He spoke about the need to "guess in the right direction." In his time, such procedure was unacceptable to the professional and scientific community. He—and we, his students—was constantly exposed to the criticism of oversimplification, of jumping to conclusions. This we did—but for good reasons. Today, guessing—following hunches—is not only proper; it is essential for "scientific" progress. In the "stochastic process" one makes an hypothesis and then one finds its validity. The law of parsimony makes it clear that the simpler the explanation of events, the greater the chance of its being correct.

Here we find Adler's greatest contribution. He not only saw man as an indivisible whole—for this reason he called his psychological system of the indivisible personality "Individual Psychology"—but he also gave us a technique to perceive man as a whole, in his movements, in his goals. It is this holistic approach that enables us to "jump to conclusions" when we perceive the whole person and his pattern. Yet while the holistic approach is gaining rapid recognition, the causalistic-deterministic thinking of the seventeenth century still affects our social and behavioral scientists.

It was the "unscientific" approach of Adler that made him despair of professional and scientific support. Consequently, he turned toward teaching lay people. Most of his books were written for them. He even went so far as to train lay people to be counselors and therapists. For many years his lay endeavors proved to be an obstacle to getting widespread support for himself and his followers. Only now, at the time of the centennial celebration of his birth, is Adler gaining long-overdue recognition.

There are several reasons for this new development. Adler's model of man fits the needs of a democratic era. His recognition of man's ability to decide is slowly but definitely replacing the prevalent concept of man's being weak and small, the victim of forces from within and from without. Adler's emphasis on the social nature of man is replacing dominant biological concepts. His holistic and teleo-analytic approach is increasingly accepted. What has before been a stumbling block is now becoming essential for correction: guidance and therapy. Man can only be understood and improved in the role he plays in a group. Group counseling and group therapy, first introduced by Adler, have become the methods of choice; family therapy has become the focal point of interest. And, finally, the training of lay people, which had been rejected in the past, is now considered a

ix

necessity. Even universities are training lay leaders to become counselors. And lay people can bring the philosophical premises of Adler to the community.

The acceptance of Adler's theory and methods poses a new obligation for his followers: not only must they prove Adler's postulates, but they must help mankind, which can benefit from the application of the Adlerian principles. Whatever Adler described as being effective in dealing with children proved its value for *all* human relationships, be they within the family, in the school, in the community, in industry or, eventually—let us hope—in politics. Social interest is recognized today as the basis for normalcy; therefore, the development of a deeper and stronger social interest is not only the goal of education, of guidance and therapy, but an indispensable prerequisite for man's ability to live in peace with his fellow man.

RUDOLF DREIKURS, M.D., Director
The Alfred Adler Institute of Chicago

THE EDUCATION OF CHILDREN

CHAPTER ONE

INTRODUCTION

FROM a psychological point of view, the problem of education reduces itself, in the case of
adults, to the problem of self-knowledge and rational self-direction. In the case of children education may be approached in the same manner, but
there is this difference: on account of the immaturity
of children, the question of guidance—never wholly
absent in the case of adults—takes on supreme importance. We could, if we wished, allow children to
develop of their own accord, and if they had twenty
thousand years or so to develop and a favorable environment, they would eventually approach the
standards of adult civilization. This method is of
course out of the question, and the adult must necessarily take an interest in guiding the child in his
development.

Here the great difficulty is ignorance. It is difficult enough for the adult to know himself, to know

3

the cause of his emotions, his likes and hates—in short, to understand his own psychology. It is doubly difficult to understand children and to guide them on the basis of proper knowledge.

Individual Psychology has specially concerned itself with the psychology of children, both on its own account and for the light it sheds on adult traits and adult behavior. And unlike other psychological approaches, it allows no gap to exist between theory and practice. It fastens on the unity of personality and studies its dynamic struggle for development and expression. From such a point of view scientific knowledge is already practical wisdom, for the knowledge is a knowledge of mistakes, and whoever has this knowledge—whether it be the psychologist, the parent, the friend or the individual himself—immediately sees its practical application in the guidance of the personality concerned.

On account of the method of approach of Individual Psychology, its doctrines hang together as an organic whole. Because it sees the behavior of individuals as motivated and directed by the unity of personality, whatever Individual Psychology has to say about human behavior reflects the same interrelation that is manifested in the activities of the psyche. In this opening chapter the attempt will therefore be made to present the viewpoint of Individual Psychology as a whole, with the later chapters undertaking to treat at fuller length the various interrelated problems that are here broached.

The fundamental fact in human development is the dynamic and purposive striving of the psyche. A child, from its earliest infancy, is engaged in a constant struggle to develop, and this struggle is in accordance with an unconsciously formed but ever-present goal—a vision of greatness, perfection and superiority. This struggle, this goal-forming activity, reflects, of course, the peculiarly human faculty of thinking and of imagining, and it dominates all our specific acts throughout life. It dominates even our thoughts, for we do not think objectively but in accordance with the goal and style of life we have formed.

The unity of personality is implicit in each human being's existence. Every individual represents both a unity of personality and the individual fashioning of that unity. The individual is thus both the picture and the artist. He is the artist of his own personality, but as an artist he is neither an infallible worker, nor a person with a complete understanding of soul and body—he is rather a weak, extremely fallible and imperfect human being.

In considering the construction of a personality, the chief defect to be noted is that its unity, its particular style and goal, is not built upon objective reality, but upon the subjective view the individual takes of the facts of life. A conception, a view of a fact, is never the fact itself, and it is for this reason that human beings, all of whom live in the same world of facts, mould themselves differently. Each one organizes himself according to his personal view of things, and some views are more sound, and some views are less sound. We must always reckon with these individual mistakes and failures in the development of a human being. Especially must we reckon with the misinterpretations made in early childhood, for these dominate the subsequent course of our existence.

A concrete instance of this may be seen in this clinical case. A woman, at the age of fifty-two, was always disparaging women that were older than herself. She related the fact that when she was a tiny child, she always felt humiliated and undervalued because of an older sister, who received all the attention. Looking at this case with what we might call the "vertical" point of view of Individual

Psychology, we can see the same mechanism, the same psychological dynamics both at the beginning of her life and at present—that is to say, near the close of her existence. There is always the fear of being undervalued and the anger and irritation at finding others favored or preferred. Even if we knew nothing else of this woman's life, or of her particular unity of personality, we could almost fill in the gaps in our knowledge on the basis of the two facts given. The psychologist acts here like a novelist, who has to construct a human being with a definite line of action, style of life, or pattern of behavior, and has to construct him in such a way that the impression of a unified personality is not disturbed. A good psychologist would be able to predict the conduct of this woman in certain situations, and to describe clearly the traits which accompany this particular "life line" in her personality.

The striving or goal-forming activity, which is responsible for the construction of individual personalities, presupposes another important psychological fact. This is the sense or feeling of inferiority. All children have an inherent feeling of inferiority which stimulates the imagination and incites attempts to dissipate the psychological sense of inferiority by bettering the situation. A bettering of one's situation results in a lessening of the feeling of inferiority. From a psychological point of view it may be regarded as a compensation.

Now the important thing about the sense of inferiority and the mechanism of psychological compensation is that it opens up a vast possibility of making mistakes. The sense of inferiority may stimulate objective accomplishment; it may also result in a purely psychological adjustment which widens the gulf between the individual and objective reality. Or, again, the sense of inferiority may appear so tragic that the only way it can be overcome is by the development of psychological compensatory traits, which in the end may not overcome the situation at all but which are nonetheless psychologically necessary and inevitable.

There are, for example, three classes of children who manifest very clearly the development of compensatory traits. They are children who come into the world with weak or imperfect organs; children who are treated with severity and with no affection; and, finally, children who receive too much pampering.

8

THE EDUCATION OF CHILDREN

We may take these three classes of children as exemplifying three basic situations in terms of which the development of the more normal types of children may be studied and understood. Not every child is born a cripple, but it is surprising how many children manifest, to a greater or lesser degree, psychological traits based on some physical difficulty or weak organ—psychological traits of which the archetype may be studied in the extreme case of the crippled child. And as for the classifications of pampered and hated children, practically all children fall to a greater or lesser degree into one, or even both.

All these three primary situations produce a feeling of insufficiency and inferiority, and by way of reaction, an ambition beyond the realm of human possibility. The sense of inferiority and the striving for superiority are always two phases of the same fundamental fact in human life, and are thus inseparable. In pathological situations, it is difficult to say whether it is the exaggerated feeling of inferiority, or the exacerbated striving for superiority which is most harmful. They both go together in more or less rhythmical waves. In the case of children we find the inordinate ambition, aroused by an exaggerated sense of inferiority, acting like a poison in the soul—forever making the child dissatisfied. Such a dissatisfaction is not one which leads to useful activity. It remains fruitless because it is fed by a disproportionate ambition. This ambition may be seen twisting itself into character traits and personal mannerisms. It acts like a perpetual irritant making the individual supersensitive and on guard lest he be hurt or trodden upon.

Types of this nature—and the annals of Individual Psychology are full of them—develop into persons whose abilities remain dormant, persons who become, as we say, "nervous," or eccentric. Persons of these types, when driven too far, wind up in the world of the irresponsible and the criminal because they think only of themselves and not of others. Their egotism, both moral and psychological, becomes absolute. We find some of them avoiding reality and objective facts and constructing a new world for themselves. By day-dreaming, by hugging imaginative fantasies as if they represented reality, they finally succeed in creating psychological peace. They have reconciled reality and the mind by constructing reality in the image of the mind.

In all such developments the tell-tale criterion which needs to be watched by the psychologist and by the parent is the degree of social feeling which the child or individual manifests. Social feeling is the crucial and deciding factor in normal development. Every disturbance which results in a lessening of the social or communal feeling has a tremendously harmful effect on the mental growth of the child. Social feeling is the barometer of the child's normality.

It is around the principle of social feeling that Individual Psychology has developed its pedagogical technique. Parents or guardians must not permit a child to attach himself to one person only. If this is permitted the child will find himself badly or insufficiently prepared for later life.

A good way of finding out the degree of social feeling of a child is to observe him at the time when he enters school. On entering school the child meets with one of his earliest and severest tests. The school is a new situation for the child: it will therefore reveal how well the child has been prepared to face new situations, and particularly how well he has been prepared to meet new persons.

It is the general lack of knowledge as to how to prepare a child for school that explains why so many adults look back on their school years as a sort of nightmare. Of course the school, when properly administered, will often make up for the deficiencies

11

in the earlier rearing of the children. The ideal school should serve as a mediator between the home and the wide world of reality, and should be a place not merely for book knowledge, but a place in which the knowledge and art of living should be taught. But while we are waiting for the ideal school to develop so that it may overcome the deficiencies in the parental education of children, we can also put our finger on the faults of the parents.

For analyzing the faults of family upbringing the school may serve as an indicator, precisely because it is not yet an ideal environment. Children who have not been taught how to make contact with others feel themselves alone when they enter school. As a result they are regarded as peculiar, and thus the initial tendency grows stronger and stronger with time. Their proper development is thwarted, and they become behavior problem children. People blame the school in such cases, although the school has here merely brought out the latent defects in the home education.

It has always been an open question to Individual Psychology whether behavior problem children can make any progress in school at all. We have always been able to prove that it is a danger sign when a child begins to fail at school. It is a sign not so much of failure in studies but of psychological failure. It means that the child has begun to lose faith in himself. Discouragement has made its appearance, and the child begins to avoid useful roads and normal tasks, searching all the time for another outlet, a road to freedom and easy success. Instead of the road which society has mapped out, he chooses a private road where he can erect a compensation for his inferiority by attaining a sense of superiority. He chooses the path that is always attractive to discouraged individuals—the path of quickest psychological success. It is easier to distinguish one's self and to give one's self the feeling of a conqueror by throwing off social and moral responsibilities and by breaking the law, than by following the established social paths. But this easy road to superiority is always an indication of underlying cowardice and weakness, no matter what apparent daring and bravery are manifested in the outward acts. Such a person always tries to do those things in which he is certain to succeed, thus showing off his superiority.

Just as we observe that criminals, despite their apparent recklessness and bravery, are at bottom cowardly, so we have been able to see how children in less dangerous situations betray their sense of weakness by various small signs. Thus we commonly see children (and for that matter adults, too) who are not able to stand upright but must always lean against something. Under the old methods of training children and the old ways of understanding such signs, the symptom was treated but not the underlying situation. One used to say to such a child, "Don't lean on something all the time." Actually what matters here is not that the child leans, but that he always feels the need of a support. One can readily persuade the child, either by punishment or reward, to give up this sign of weakness, but his great need for support is not thereby relieved. The disease continues. It is a good educator who can read signs and can eradicate the underlying disease with sympathy and understanding.

From a single sign one can often draw conclusions as to the presence of many qualities or traits. In the case of a child obsessed with the need of leaning on something, we can see at once that such traits as anxiety and dependence are sure to be present. By comparing him with similar persons whose cases we know thoroughly, we can reconstruct such a personality, and we can see, in short, that we have to deal with a pampered child.

We turn now to the character traits of another class of children—those who have gone without love.

The traits of this class, in their most developed form, can be observed by studying the biographies of all the great enemies of humanity. In all the life stories of these men the one thing that stands out is the fact that as children they were badly treated. In this way they developed a hardness of character, envy and hatred. They could not bear to see others happy. Now, envious persons of this type are found not merely among straight villains but among supposedly normal persons. Such individuals when they have charge of children think that the children should not be any happier than they themselves were as children. We find such a view applied by parents to their children, as well as by guardians to the children of others who are put in their charge.

Such a view, such thoughts, do not spring from bad intentions. They simply reflect the mentality of those who have been harshly brought up. Such persons can produce any number of good reasons and maxims, as for example, "Spare the rod and spoil the child!" And they give us endless proofs and examples, which do not quite convince us inasmuch as the futility of a rigid, authoritative education is proved by the simple fact that it estranges the child from his educator.

By exploring various symptoms and interrelating them, the psychologist can, after some practice, organize a system by the aid of which the hidden psychological processes of an individual may be revealed. While every point which we examine by this system reflects something of the complete personality of the individual under investigation, we can feel satisfied only when we get the same indications at every point of our examination. Individual Psychology is thus an art as well as a science, and it cannot be too much emphasized that the speculative scheme, the system of concepts, is not to be applied in a wooden and mechanical fashion to an individual under examination. In all investigations the primary thing is to study the individual; we must never draw far-reaching conclusions from one or two modes of expression, but we must look for all possible supporting phases. Only when we are successful in confirming our tentative hypothesis, only when we have been able, for example, to find the same stubbornness and discouragement in other aspects of his behavior, can we say with certainty that this stubbornness or discouragement permeates the entire personality.

In this connection it must be remembered that the subject under examination has no understanding of his own forms of expression and is thus unable to conceal his true self. We see his personality in action, and his personality is revealed not by what he says or thinks about himself but by his acts interpreted in their context. It is not that the patient deliberately wants to lie to us, but we have learned to recognize a vast gulf between a man's conscious thoughts and his unconscious motivations—a gulf which can best be bridged by a disinterested but sympathetic outsider. The outsider—whether he be the psychologist, or the parent or the teacher—should learn to interpret a personality on the basis of objective facts seen as the expression of the purposive, but more or less unconscious, strivings of the individual.

Thus the attitude of the individual with regard to the three fundamental questions of individual and social life reveals his true self as nothing else can. The first of these questions is the social relation, which we have already discussed in the context of the contrast between the private and objective views of reality. But the social relation manifests itself also as a specific task—it is the task of making friends and getting along with people. How does the individual meet that problem? What is his answer? When a human being believes he can evade the question by saying that the matter of friends, the matter of social relationships is of complete indifference to him, then indifference is his answer. From this indifference we can, of course, draw conclusions as to the direction and organization of his personality. It is to be noted, moreover, that the social relation is not confined merely to the physical making of friends and meeting of people: all the abstract qualities like friendship, comradeship, truthfulness and loyalty cluster about this relation, and the answer to the social relation indicates the individual's answer on all these points.

The second great question concerns how the individual wants to make use of his life—what part he wants to take in the general division of labor. If the social question may be said to be determined by the existence of more than one ego, by the relationship I-you, then we may say that this question is determined by the fundamental relationship Man-Earth. If one could reduce all mankind into one person, this person would have mutuality with the earth. What does he want from the earth? Just as in the case of the first question, the solution of the problem of occupation is not a one-sided or private matter, but a matter between man and earth. It is a two-sided relationship in which man hasn't got it all his own way.

18

Success is determined not by our private will but in relation to objective realities. For this reason the answer that an individual makes, and the manner in which he makes it, to the question of occupation throws a very revealing light on his personality and on his attitude towards life.

The third fundamental question arises from the fact that mankind is divided into two sexes. The solution of this problem is again not a private, subjective matter, but must be solved according to the inherent objective logic of the relationship. What is my position towards the other sex? The typical private conception is again a mistaken conception. A correct solution can be arrived at only through a careful consideration of all the questions which cluster around the sex relationship. And it stands to reason that every departure from a correct solution of the problem of love and marriage indicates a mistake, an error in the personality. Also many of the harmful consequences that follow a wrong solution of this problem are to be interpreted in the light of the underlying error of personality.

We can see, therefore, that we are in a position to discover the general style of life and particular goal of an individual from the way in which he answers these three questions. The goal is omnipotent. It decides a person's style of life and it will be reflected in every one of his acts. Thus if the goal is a striving towards being a fellow man, a goal directed to the useful side of life, the stamp of that goal will be apparent in the individual's solutions of all his problems. All the solutions will reflect constructive usefulness, and the individual will have the sense of happiness and the feeling of worth and power that go with constructive and useful activity. If the goal is directed otherwise, if it is directed to the private and useless side of life, the individual will find himself unable to solve fundamental problems, and he will also lack the joy that comes from their proper solution.

There is a strong interconnection between all these fundamental problems, and it is made all the stronger by the fact that in the course of social life specific tasks spring out of these fundamental problems which can be carried out properly only in a social or communal setting, or, in other words, on the basis of social feeling. These tasks begin in the earliest years of childhood, when our sense-organs are developing in accordance with the stimulus of social life, in looking, speaking, hearing—in our relations to our brothers, sisters, parents, relatives, acquaintances, comrades, friends and teachers. They continue through life in the same manner, so that he who gets out of social touch with his fellows is lost.

And so Individual Psychology stands on firm ground when it regards as "right" that which is useful for the community. It realizes that every departure from the social standard is an offense against right and brings with it a conflict with the objective laws and objective necessities of reality. This clash with objectivity makes itself felt first of all in the feeling of worthlessness on the part of the offending individual, and it also comes out—with even stronger force—in the retaliations of the others who feel themselves aggrieved. Finally, it may be said, that the departure from the social standard violates an immanent social ideal which every one of us, consciously or unconsciously, carries in himself.

With its rigorous emphasis on social-mindedness as a test of development, Individual Psychology finds it easy to understand and evaluate the style of life of any child. For as soon as the child is confronted with a life problem, he will reveal, as if he were under examination, whether or not he has been "rightly" prepared. He will show, in other words, whether he has social feeling, whether he has courage, under-

21

standing, and in general a useful goal. What we then try to find out is the form and rhythm of his upward striving, the degree of his feeling of inferiority, the intensity of his social consciousness. All these things are closely interconnected and interpenetrate one another so as to form an organic and unbreakable unity—a unity that is unbreakable until the fault of construction is discovered and a reconstruction is accomplished.

CHAPTER TWO

THE UNITY OF PERSONALITY

T HE psychic life of a child is a wonderful thing, and it fascinates at every point where one touches it. Perhaps the most remarkable fact of all is the way in which one must unroll the whole scroll of the child's life in order to understand a single event. Every act seems to express the whole of a child's life and personality, and is thus unintelligible without a knowledge of this invisible background. To this phenomenon we give the name unity of personality.

The development of this unity—the co-ordination of actions and expressions into a single pattern— begins at a very early age. The demands of life compel the child to make his responses in a unified manner, and this unified manner of answering situations is not only what constitutes the child's character but individualizes each of his acts and makes them distinct from the similar acts of other children.

This fact of the unity of personality is generally

overlooked by most schools of psychology; or, if it is not entirely overlooked, it does not receive in their hands the attention that it deserves. As a result we often find both in psychological theory and in psychiatrical technique a particular gesture or a particular expression singled out for consideration as if it were an independent entity. Sometimes such a manifestation is called a complex, and the assumption is that it is possible to separate it from the rest of an individual's activity. But such a procedure is comparable to singling out one note from an entire melody and attempting to understand the significance of this one note apart from the string of notes which make up the melody. The procedure is an improper one, but unfortunately it is widespread.

Individual Psychology is compelled to take a stand against this widespread error, which is especially harmful when it is applied to the education of children. In that connection it expresses itself in the theory of punishment. What happens generally when a child does something that invites punishment? It is true that in a certain sense the total impression made by the child's personality is usually taken into account, but this is more often a disadvantage than otherwise, since in the case of an oft-repeated mistake the teacher or parent is apt to be prejudiced in approaching the child and regards him as incorrigible. It is also true that on the basis of a total impression one is apt to deal less harshly with the mistakes of a child whose behavior is otherwise quite good. Nonetheless in neither instance do we reach the real root of the problem as we should on the basis of the total comprehension of the child's unity of personality. We are in the position of trying to understand the significance of a few individual notes torn from the context of the whole melody.

When we ask a child why he is lazy, we cannot expect him to know the basic connection which it is essential for us to know. Neither can we expect him to tell us why he lies. For thousands of years the saying of Socrates, who had so great an understanding of human nature, has been sounding in our ears: "How difficult it is to know one's self!" By what right, then, can we demand that a child answer such complex questions, the solution of which is difficult even for a psychologist? To be able to understand the significance of individual expression presupposes having a method for understanding the whole personality. This does not mean a description of what he does and how he acts, but involves understanding the child's attitude towards the tasks which lie before him.

THE EDUCATION OF CHILDREN

The following example shows how essential it is that we understand the whole context of a child's life. A boy of thirteen was the older of two children. He was for five years the only child of parents who had seen better days. Then a sister was born. Previously every person in his environment was only too glad to fulfill every desire the boy had. The mother undoubtedly pampered him. The father was a good-natured, tranquil sort of person, who enjoyed his son's dependence on him. The son, naturally, was closer to his mother, since the father was an army officer and frequently away from home. Now the mother was a clever and well-meaning woman, who tried to satisfy every whim of her dependent but insistent son. Nonetheless she was often annoyed at a display of ill-breeding or threatening gestures. A state of tension was created, and this tension expressed itself chiefly in the boy's constantly trying to tyrannize his mother—ordering her about, teasing her, and in short making himself disagreeably prominent wherever and whenever he could.

The boy's conduct was very troublesome to his mother, but since there were no other particularly bad features, she yielded to him, kept his clothes in order and helped him with his school work. The boy was always confident that his mother would help him out of any difficulty he got into. He was undoubtedly an intelligent child, just as well educated as the average, and he went through elementary school with fair success until his eighth year. At that time a great transformation took place which made the relation of the child to his parents unendurable. Not only did he drive his mother wild by his complete neglect of himself and by personal carelessness in connection with all bodily functions, but he would pull his mother's hair whenever she did not give him what he wanted; he never left her in peace, always pinching her ear or pulling her hand. He refused to abandon his tactics, and as his baby sister grew up, he clung all the more to the behavior pattern he had devised. His little sister soon became the target of his tricks. Not that he went so far as to harm the child physically, but his jealousy of her was clearly apparent. His great deterioration dates from the time his sister was born and began to play a role in the family constellation.

It needs to be particularly emphasized that in such a situation, when a child's behavior grows worse, or certain new unpleasant symptoms make their appearance, we must take into consideration not only the time when the condition started but also the stimulating cause. The word cause must be used re-

luctantly, since one cannot see why the birth of a
sister should be a reason for an older brother's becoming a problem child. Nonetheless this happens
frequently, and this relationship cannot be regarded
other than as a mistaken attitude on the part of the
child. It is not a matter of causality in the strict
physical-scientific sense, for it cannot be claimed
that *because* a younger child is born the older one
must deteriorate. It may be asserted that when a
stone falls to the ground, it must fall in a certain
direction and with a certain speed. But the investigations made by Individual Psychology give it the
right to claim that in a psychic "fall" strict causality
does not play a role—only bigger or smaller mistakes which, after they are made, affect the future
development of the individual.

It is no cause for wonder that in the development
of the human psyche mistakes should appear, and
that these mistakes and their consequences should
lie side by side and reveal themselves in some failure
or wrong orientation. All this is due to the goal-
setting activity of the psyche, and this goal-setting
involves judgment—that is to say, the possibility
of making mistakes. This setting or determining of
a goal commences in the earliest years. In his second
or third year, as a rule, the child begins to fix for

himself a goal of superiority which is forever before him and towards which he strives in his own manner. Now the fixing of the goal usually involves incorrect judgment; nonetheless it is more or less binding on the child. The child concretizes his goal, in his specific acts and arranges his entire life, so that it becomes a constant striving towards this goal.

We see, then, how important it is to bear in mind that a child's development is determined by his personal, individual interpretation of things; how important to realize that the child always behaves in the circle of his personal mistakes whenever he approaches a new and difficult situation. We know that the depth or character of the impression which the situation makes upon the child does not depend upon the objective fact or circumstance (as for example the birth of a second child), but depends rather on how this child regards the fact. This is sufficient ground for refuting the theory of causality: necessary connection exists between objective facts and their absolute meaning, but not between mistaken views of facts.

What is truly remarkable about our psychic life is that it is our points of view which decide the directions we take, and not the facts themselves. This is an extraordinarily important circumstance, inasmuch as all our activities are regulated and our personality is organized on the basis of it. A classic example of this play of subjective ideas in human action is furnished by Cæsar's landing in Egypt. As he jumped ashore he stumbled and fell on the ground, and the Roman soldiers took this as an unfavorable omen. Brave as they were, they would nonetheless have turned around and gone back, had not Cæsar thrown out his arms and cried out, "I have you, Africa!" We can see from this how little the structure of reality is causal, and how its effects can be moulded and determined by an organized and well-integrated personality. The same thing holds true with regard to mob psychology and its relations to reason: if a condition of mob psychology gives way to common sense, it is not because either the mob psychology or common sense reason were causally determined by the situation, but because both represent spontaneous points of view. Usually common sense does not make its appearance until after mistaken points of view have been tried out.

Coming back to the story of the boy, we may say that he soon found himself in a difficult situation. No one liked him any more, he made no progress at school and yet he continued to behave in the same way. His behavior, which was continually disturbing to others, had become a complete expression of his personality. And so what happened? Whenever he disturbed some one, he was immediately punished. He would get a bad report card or else a letter of complaint would be sent to his parents. Things went on in this way until at length his parents were advised to remove the boy from school, since he did not seem suited for school life.

Probably nobody was happier than the boy at such a solution. He did not want anything else. The logical consistency of his behavior pattern revealed itself again in his attitude. It was a mistaken attitude, but once assumed it expressed itself consistently. He had made his basic mistake when he had set for himself the goal of always being the center of attention. And if he was to be punished for any mistake, this is the mistake for which he should have been punished. It was as a result of this mistake that he tried constantly to make his mother wait on him. And it was as a result of this mistake, too, that he acted like a king who, after eight years of absolute power, is suddenly deprived of his throne. Up to the moment of his dethronement he had been the only one who existed for his mother, and she for him. Then his sister arrived, and he struggled violently to recover his lost throne. That was again his mistake, but one must grant that such a blunder does not involve any inherent badness or viciousness. Viciousness first develops when a child is brought into a situation for which he is totally unprepared, and is allowed to struggle without any guidance. Take a child, for example, who has been prepared only for a situation in which some one devotes herself entirely to him: suddenly the contrary is true. The child is at school, where the teacher must divide his attention among many, and is rather annoyed when one child demands more than his proportionate share. Such a situation is full of danger for the pampered child, but at the outset the child is far from being vicious or incorrigible.

It is understandable that in the case of the boy a conflict should have developed between his personal scheme of existence and the scheme of existence demanded by the school. The conflict may be represented diagrammatically by picturing the direction and the goal of the child's personality and the goal set by school life. The goals point in diverging directions. But everything that happens in the child's life is determined by his goal, and there is no motion, so to speak, in his whole system except in the direction of this goal. On the other hand the school expects a normal scheme of existence for every child. The conflict is inevitable, but the school fails to appreciate the psychological facts in the situation and neither makes any allowances for it nor attempts to obviate the source of the conflict.

We know that the child's life is motivated by the dominant desire to make his mother serve him and him alone. In his psychological scheme of existence everything may be said to converge on this thought: I must dominate my mother, I must be the only one to possess her. But other things are expected of him. It is expected of him that he work alone, that he take care of his school books and papers, and that he keep his possessions in order. It is as if one hitched a fiery race horse to a truck wagon.

Of course the boy's performance in such a case is not of the highest, but when we know what the real circumstances are we are much more inclined to be sympathetic. It is no use to punish the boy in school, because that would definitely convince him that school is no place for him. When he is expelled from school, or when the parents are asked to take him away, the boy is that much nearer to his goal. His false scheme of apperception acts like a trap. He feels that he has gained, because he now really has

33

his mother in his power. She must again devote herself exclusively to him. And that is just what he wants.

When we recognize the true state of affairs we must admit that it is of no use to pick one fault or another and punish the child for it. Suppose for example that he forgets a book—it would be a wonder if he didn't, for when he forgets it he gives his mother something to do. It is not an isolated individual act, it is part of the whole scheme of personality. When we bear in mind that all the expressions of a personality are consistent parts of a whole, we can see that this boy is acting simply in accordance with his style of life. And the fact that he acts consistently, in accordance with the logic of his personality, at the same time disproves any presumption that his inability to perform his school tasks is due to feeble-mindedness. A feeble-minded person is unable to follow out his own style of life.

This highly complex case brings up still another point. We are all of us in a somewhat similar situation to that of this boy. Our own schemes, our own interpretations of life are never in complete harmony with the received social tradition. In the old days one looked upon the social tradition as sacrosanct; now we have come to realize, however, that there is nothing sacred or fixed about the social institutions of humanity. They are all in process of development, and the motive power in that process is the struggle of the individuals within society. Social institutions exist for the sake of the individual, and not the individual for the sake of social institutions. The salvation of the individual lies indeed in being social-minded, but social-mindedness does not imply forcing the individual into a Procrustean social mould.

Such considerations on the relation of the individual to society, which lie at the basis of the doctrines of Individual Psychology, apply with special force to the school system and its treatment of maladjusted children. The school must learn to regard the child as a personality, as a value to be cultivated and developed, and at the same time it must learn to use psychological insight in judging particular acts. It must regard these particular acts, as we have said, not as single notes but in the context of the whole melody—the unity of personality.

CHAPTER THREE

THE STRIVING FOR SUPERIORITY AND ITS EDUCATIONAL SIGNIFICANCE

NEXT to the unity of personality the most important psychological fact about human nature is the striving for superiority and success. This striving is of course directly related to the feeling of inferiority, for if we did not feel inferior we should not have any desire to go beyond the immediate situation. The two problems—the desire for superiority and the sense of inferiority—are really two phases of the same psychological phenomenon, but for purposes of exposition it is convenient to treat them more or less separately. In this chapter we shall try to confine ourselves to the striving for superiority and its educational consequences.

The first question that one may ask about the striving for superiority is whether it is innate, like our biological instincts. The answer we must give is that this is a highly improbable supposition. We cannot really speak of the superiority striving as in any definite sense inborn. However, we must admit that a substrate must exist—there must be an embryonic core with the possibilities of development. Perhaps we may put it best this way: human nature is tied up with the development of the striving for superiority.

We know, of course, that human activities are confined within certain bounds, and that there are abilities which we can never develop. For example, we can never attain the smell faculty of a dog; nor is it possible to perceive with our eyes the ultra-violet rays of the spectrum. But there are certain functional abilities which can be developed further, and it is in this possibility of further development that we see the biological root of the striving for superiority and the whole source of the psychological unfolding of personality.

As far as we can see, this dynamic urge to assert one's self under all circumstances is common both to children and adults. There is no way of exterminating it. Human nature does not tolerate permanent submission; humanity has even overthrown its gods. The feeling of degradation and depreciation, the mood of uncertainty and of inferiority always give rise to a desire for reaching a higher level in order to obtain compensation and completeness.

We can show that certain peculiarities of children

betray the work of environmental forces which develop in them feelings of inferiority, weakness and uncertainty, which in turn exercise a stimulating influence upon their whole mental life. They make it their aim to free themselves from this condition, to reach a higher level and to gain a feeling of equality. The more stormy the upward aspirations are, the higher the child sets his aims, looking for proofs of his strength—proofs which often transcend the limits of human powers. Because of the support that he sometimes obtains from various quarters, the child is enabled to project a picture of the future bordering on God. In one way or another the imagination of children is apt to betray the fact that they are possessed with the idea of divine resemblance. This generally occurs in children who feel weakest.

There is the case of a child of fourteen years who found himself in a very bad mental situation. When he was asked for childhood impressions, he remembered how painful it was for him to realize that he was unable to whistle at the age of six. One day, however, as he came out of his house he succeeded in whistling. He was so surprised that he believed that it was God who whistled in him. This shows clearly that there is an intimate and close connection between the feeling of weakness on the one hand and the nearness of God on the other.

This aspiration for superiority is connected with striking character traits. By observing this tendency we witness the whole ambition of such a child. When this desire for self-assertion becomes extraordinarily intense, it will also always involve an element of envy. Children of this type easily develop the habit of wishing their competitors all kinds of evils; and not only wishing—which often leads to neurosis—but also doing harm, causing trouble, and even manifesting now and then downright criminal traits. Such a child can slander, betray domestic secrets and degrade the other fellow so as to feel that his own value is enhanced, especially when he is being observed by others. No one is supposed to surpass him, therefore it does not matter to him whether he himself rises or the other fellow sinks in value. When the desire for power becomes very strong, it expresses itself in malevolence, vindictiveness. These children will always display a militant and defiant attitude, which will show itself in their external appearance —in the flashing of their eyes, in their sudden outbursts of anger, in their readiness to fight imaginary foes. To be submitted to a test is, for children aiming at superiority, an extremely painful situation, for in this way their worthlessness might easily be exposed.

This fact shows that it is necessary to adapt the tests to the peculiarities of the child. A test does not mean the same thing to every child. We can often find children for whom a test is a highly burdensome event, who blush and turn pale, begin to stutter and tremble, who are so paralyzed by shame and fear that their minds become blank. Some can answer only in unison with others, otherwise they cannot answer at all because they suspect that they are being watched. This desire for superiority will also manifest itself in plays. An intense desire for superiority in this direction will not allow the child to play the part of a horse at the time when others appear as drivers. He will always want to be the driver himself, he will always attempt to lead and direct. But when he is kept back by past experience from assuming such a role, he will content himself with disturbing the games of others. And if he is still further discouraged by numerous defeats, his ambition will be thwarted, and any new situation will drive him back instead of stimulating him to go forward.

Ambitious children who have not yet been discouraged will display inclinations for competitive games of all kinds, and they will equally manifest consternation in case of defeat. The degree and direction of the desire for self-assertion can often be inferred from favorite games, tales, historical figures, persons. In the case of adults we often find the worship of Napoleon, who is highly fit to serve as a model for ambitious people. Megalomania in day-dreaming is always a sign of a strong feeling of inferiority which stimulates disappointed people to look for satisfaction and intoxication in feelings produced outside of reality. Something similar often takes place in dreams.

In observing the different directions which children take in their striving for superiority, variations become apparent which we can divide into certain types. We cannot make this type division a precise one because the variations are innumerable, and are determined primarily by the amount of confidence the child has in himself. Children whose development has not been hindered direct this striving for superiority into the channels of useful accomplishment; they try to please their teachers, to be orderly, to develop into normal school youngsters. We know from our experience, however, that these cases are not in the majority.

There are also children who want to excel others

and who manifest a suspicious intensity in their struggle to surpass. Frequently there is a note of exaggerated ambition in such a striving which is easily overlooked because we are accustomed to regard ambition as a virtue and to stimulate the child to further effort. This is usually a mistake because the development of a child suffers from too much ambition. A swollen ambition produces a state of tension which the child can bear for a while, but inevitably there will be signs that the tension is growing too great. The child may spend too much time at home with his books and his other activities will suffer. Such children frequently avoid other problems solely on account of their eagerness to be ahead in school. We cannot be completely satisfied with such a development since a child cannot thrive mentally and physically under such circumstances.

The way in which such a child arranges his life to be able to surpass all others is not best suited to a normal growth. There comes a time when he must be told not to spend so much time with his books, to go out into the air, to play with his friends and occupy himself with other things. Such children are likewise not in the majority, but they occur frequently enough.

In addition, it often happens that there are two pupils in a class between whom there is a tacit rivalry. He who has the opportunity to observe closely will find that such competing children occasionally develop traits which are not particularly agreeable. They become envious and jealous, qualities which certainly do not belong to an independent, harmonious personality. They are annoyed at the successes of other children, they commence to have nervous headaches, stomach aches, etc., when some one else forges ahead. They withdraw to one side when another child is praised, and of course they will never be able to praise somebody else. This is a sign of envy which does not throw such a good light upon exaggerated ambition.

Such children do not get along well with their comrades. They want the leading part in everything and are unwilling to subordinate themselves to the general organization of a game. The result is that they do not like to play in company and act haughtily toward their schoolmates. Every contact with their schoolmates is to them unpleasant; the more so, the more insecure they believe their position to be. Such children are never sure of their success and are easily rattled when they feel themselves in an insecure atmosphere. They are overburdened by the expectations which others have in regard to them, and also by their own expectations of themselves.

The expectations that the families have of such children are felt very keenly by the children themselves. They go about fulfilling every task that is set before them with excitement and nervousness because they have always before their eyes the vision of surpassing all others, of being a "shining light." They feel the weight of the hopes which rest on them, and they will carry this weight only so long as circumstances are favorable.

If human beings were blessed with absolute truth and were able to find a perfect method which would spare children such difficulties, we should probably have no behavior problem children. Since we do not have such a method, and since the conditions under which children must learn cannot be ideally arranged, it is obvious that the anxious expectations of such children are an extraordinarily dangerous matter. They will face a difficulty with quite different feelings from those which other children have who are not burdened with such unhealthy ambition. By difficulties we mean those which are unavoidable. It is and probably always will be impossible to prevent a child from encountering difficulties. This is partly due to our methods which are in need of further development, which do not suit every child, and which we are constantly seeking to improve. It is also due to the fact that the confidence which children have in themselves is undermined by an exaggerated ambition. Difficulties are not faced with the courage necessary to overcome them.

Over-ambitious children are concerned only with the end result which is the recognition accorded their success. The success itself does not satisfy without the recognition. We know that in many cases it is much more important for a child to maintain his mental balance when difficulties present themselves than actually to attempt to conquer these difficulties at once. A child who has been forced into such an ambitious direction does not know this, and feels it is impossible to live without the admiration of others. The result is everywhere observable in the number of people dependent upon the opinion of others.

How important it is not to lose the sense of balance in the matter of values is shown by the example of those children who come into the world with organ inferiorities. Such cases are, of course, quite common. Many children are better developed on the left than on the right side; this is a fact which is usually unknown. A left-handed child has many difficulties in our right-handed civilization. It is necessary to use certain methods to discover whether a child is right or left-handed. Almost without exception we find left-handed children among those who have exceptional difficulty in writing, reading and drawing, and who are generally awkward with their hands. One simple, but not entirely conclusive method for finding out whether a child is congenitally right- or left-handed, is to ask the child to cross his hands. Left-handed children usually cross their hands so that the left thumb lies over the right. It is astounding to see how many people are born left-handed and have never known it.

When we investigate the history of a large number of left-handed children, we find the following facts: first, that such children were usually regarded as clumsy or awkward (which is no wonder in our right-handed arrangement of things). To understand the situation, it is only necessary to think how perplexing it is, when we have been accustomed to right-handed traffic, to attempt to cross the street in a town where traffic is to the left (England, for example, or Argentina). A left-handed child finds himself in an even worse situation in a family where all the others are right-handed. His left-handedness disturbs both the family and himself. When he learns to write in school, he finds himself below the average. As the reason is not understood, he is scolded, receives bad marks, and is often punished. The child cannot interpret his situation otherwise than to believe that he is in some way less capable than the others. A feeling will grow in him of having been curtailed, of being in some way inferior, or of not being able to compete with the others. Since he is scolded at home also for his clumsiness, he sees there only a confirmation of his inferiority.

Naturally the child does not have to accept this as a final defeat, but there are many children who give up the struggle under such disheartening conditions. Since they do not understand the real situation and no one explains to them how to overcome their difficulties, it is hard for them to keep on fighting. Many people, on this account, have an illegible handwriting because they have never trained their right hands sufficiently. That this obstacle can be overcome is proven by the fact that one finds left-handed persons among the best artists and painters, and also among script engravers. These persons have developed an ability to use their right hands simply by force of training despite their congenital left-handedness.

There is a superstition that all left-handed persons who are trained to use their right hand become stutterers. This superstition is explained by the fact that the difficulties put in the way of such children are sometimes so great that they may lose their courage to speak. That is also why there is such an unusual number of left-handed persons to be found among those who manifest other forms of discouragement (neurotics, suicides, criminals, perverse individuals, etc.). On the other hand, one often finds that those people who have overcome their left-handedness have also achieved high rank in life, frequently in an artistic atmosphere.

No matter how insignificant the single characteristic of left-handedness may appear, it still teaches us something of great importance: namely, that we can determine nothing of the ability of a child until we have brought his courage and perseverance up to a certain point. When we frighten the children, take away from them the hope of a better future, it may still appear to us that they are capable of carrying on. But if we were to increase their courage, such children would be capable of accomplishing much more.

Children with inordinate ambition are in a bad situation because it is customary to judge them by their success and not according to their preparedness to face difficulties and to combat them. It is also customary in our present form of civilization to be much more concerned with visible success than with thorough education. We know how perishable is that success which comes to us with little effort. It can therefore be of no advantage to train a child to be ambitious. It is much more important to train him to be courageous, persevering and self-confident, to recognize that failure should never discourage, but should be tackled as a new problem. It would certainly be much easier if the teacher were able to recognize at what point a child's efforts seemed futile and also whether the child made sufficient effort in the first place.

We see, therefore, that a striving for superiority can express itself in a character trait like ambition. There are children whose striving for superiority originally took the form of ambition, but who relinquished this ambition as unattainable because another child had already gotten so very much further ahead. Many teachers follow the practice of treating children who do not manifest sufficient ambition very severely, or giving them bad marks in order to arouse their dormant ambition. Occasionally this method is successful if there is still some courage left in the child. However, this method is not to be recommended for general use. Children already close to the danger line in their studies become completely confused and are driven into a state of apparent stupidity by such treatment.

On the other hand, we are often astounded at the unsuspected intelligence and capability which children manifest after having been handled with gentleness, care and understanding. It is true that children who change in this fashion frequently exhibit a greater ambition. This is simply because they are afraid of falling back to the old state. Their old way of living and the past lack of accomplishment remain before their eyes like warning signals and continually urge them forward. In later life many of them behave as if possessed by a demon; they occupy themselves day and night, suffer constantly from the effects of overwork, and believe that they are never doing enough.

All this becomes much clearer when we keep in mind the dominant idea of Individual Psychology that every individual's personality (child as well as adult) is a unified whole, and that it always expresses itself in accordance with the behavior pattern which he has gradually built up. To judge an act detached from the personality of the actor is wrong because a specific and single act can be interpreted in many ways. The uncertainty in judging vanishes at once when we comprehend the particular act or gesture—for example, tardiness—as the inevitable answer of the child to the tasks set him by the school. It means simply that he would rather have nothing to do with the school, and consequently that he does not bother to fulfill the school's requirements. In fact he does what he can in order not to comply with them.

From this standpoint we can see the whole picture of the "bad" school child. We see the tragedy that takes place when the striving for superiority expresses itself not in the acceptance of school but in the rejection of it. A series of typical behavior symptoms appear and gradually these symptoms approach closer and closer to incorrigibility and retrogradation. The child may turn into the type like the court jester. He constantly plays pranks to make others laugh and does little else. Or he may annoy his comrades. Or else he plays truant and falls in with evil companions.

We see, then, how not only does the fate of the school child lie in our hands, but the later development of the individual as well. The education and training furnished by the school determine in a crucial fashion the future life of the individual. The school is placed in between the family and life in society. It has the opportunity of correcting the mistaken styles of life formed under family upbringing, and it has the responsibility of preparing the child's adjustment to social life and of seeing to it that the child will play his individual role harmoniously in the orchestral pattern of society.

When we view the role of the school historically we see that it has always tried to turn out individuals according to the social ideal of the time. It was successively an aristocratic, religious, bourgeois and democratic school, always educating the children according to what the times and the rulers demanded. To-day in accordance with the changing social ideal the school must change also. Thus if to-day the ideal adult human being is typified by the independent, self-controlled and courageous man or woman, the school must regulate itself so that it will turn out individuals approaching that ideal.

In other words the school must not regard itself as an end in itself and must keep in mind that the individual must be trained for society and not for the school. Thus it must not neglect the children who have given up the ideal of being model children at school. These children do not necessarily have less of a striving for superiority. They can turn their attention to other things where they do not have to strain themselves, and where they believe, either rightly or wrongly, that success is easier to achieve. This may be due to the fact that they have unconsciously trained themselves in their earlier years for other activities. Thus they may not become brilliant mathematicians, but they may distinguish themselves in athletics. The educator should never dismiss any such salient accomplishment but should use it as a point of departure to encourage the child to improve in other spheres of activity. The educator's task is much easier when he starts with a single encouraging accomplishment and uses it to make the child believe he can be just as successful in other things. It is enticing the child, as it were, from one fruitful pasture to another. And since all children, except those who are feeble-minded, are quite capable of coping successfully with their school work, what needs to be overcome is simply an artificially constructed barrier. This barrier arises from taking abstract school performance, instead of the ultimate educational and social goal, as the basis for judgment. On the child's side the barrier is reflected in a lack of self-confidence, with the result that the child's striving for superiority may bring out a break with useful activity because it does not find its proper expression.

What does the child do in such a situation? He thinks of a way of escape. Often we may find him assuming some peculiarity which does not actually draw praise from the teacher, but which may attract the teacher's attention, or may only arouse the admiration of the other children at such a display of impertinence or stubbornness. Such a child, by virtue of the disturbance he creates, often regards himself as a hero, and as a little giant.

Such psychological manifestations and deviations from proper conduct arise in the course of the school experiment. Their origin cannot be traced altogether to the school, although it is in school that they come to the surface. The school, taken in a passive sense, that is to say, apart from its active educational and corrective mission, is an experiment station where the defects of the early family upbringing are brought to light.

A good and watchful teacher can see many things the first day a child is in school. For many children show at once all the signs of a pampered child to whom the new situation (the school) is most painful and disagreeable. Such a child has had no practice in making contacts with others, and it is essential that he be able to make friends. It is better and preferable that a child bring with him to school some knowledge of how to establish contact with others. He must not be dependent upon one person to the exclusion of all others. The fault of family upbringing must be corrected at school, but it is of course better that he come to the school more or less free from such a fault.

A child who has been pampered at home cannot be expected to be suddenly able to concentrate on his work at school. Such a child is not attentive. He will manifest a desire to remain at home rather than go to school—in fact he will have no "school sense." It is easy to detect the signs of this aversion to school. Thus the parents have to coax the child to get up in the morning; they must constantly urge him to do this or that; they will find him dawdling over breakfast, and so on. It would seem as if such a child has constructed an impassable barrier to prevent his making progress.

The cure, the remedy for the situation, is the same as with left-handed persons: we must give such children time to learn, and we must not punish them when they come late to school because that only increases their sense of unhappiness at school. Such punishment is regarded by the child as confirmatory of his feeling that he does not belong in school. When parents whip a child in order to force him to go to school, the child will not only not want to attend school, but will look for means to make his position more bearable. These means will, of course, be means of escape, not means of actually meeting the difficulty. The child's aversion to school, his inability to cope with the school problem will be apparent in every gesture and in every movement. He will never have his books together and will always be forgetting or losing them. When a child makes a habit of forgetting and losing books we may be certain that he is not on very good terms with his school.

In examining such children one finds almost invariably that they had no hope of being able to achieve any measure of success at school. This self-undervaluation is not entirely their own fault. The environment has helped them along in this mistaken direction. At home some one in anger has prophesied a dark future, or has called them stupid or worthless. When these children find at school what appears to be a confirmation of such accusations, they lack the judgment, the power of analysis (which their elders often also lack) to correct their misinterpretation. They thus give up the battle before they even make an attempt at combat, and they consider the defeat which they themselves bring about as an insurmountable obstacle and as a confirmation of their inability or inferiority.

Since circumstances are usually such that, once a mistake is made, there is little possibility of having the mistake corrected, and since these children usually lag behind in spite of their apparent efforts to forge ahead, they soon give up the effort and turn their attention to inventing excuses for staying away from school. Absence from school, that is to say, truancy, is one of the most dangerous symptoms. It is regarded as one of the worst sins, and the punishment is usually drastic. Thereupon the children believe themselves compelled to take refuge in cunning and in misrepresentation. There still remain a few paths which lead them into further misdeeds. They can forge notes from home and falsify report cards. They can spin a net of lies at home about all they are supposed to be doing at school, which place they have not attended for some time. They also have to find a place to hide during school hours. It goes without saying that they usually find in such hiding places other children who have already trodden this path. And so the children's striving for superiority remains unsatisfied after merely playing truant—it urges them to further acts, that is to say, to law-breaking. They go further and further, ending up with full-fledged criminality. They form gangs, they begin to steal, they learn sexual perversions, and they feel themselves quite grown up.

The great step having been taken, they now search for more food for their ambition. Inasmuch as they have remained undetected in their acts, they feel that they can commit the most cunning of crimes. This explains why so many children will not give up their life of crime. They want to go further in their development along that road because they believe that they can never achieve success in any other direction. They have excluded everything which might stimulate them to useful activity. Their ambition, continually stimulated by the deeds of their comrades, drives them to new a-social or anti-social acts. One never finds a child with criminal tendencies who is not at the same time extremely conceited. This conceit has the same source as ambition, and it forces the child continually to distinguish himself in some way or other. And when he cannot make a place for himself on the useful side of life, he turns to the useless side.

There is the case of a boy who killed his teacher. If we examine the case we find all the characteristic traits in this boy. It is a boy who had a careful but too nervous an upbringing under the guidance of a governess who believed that she knew everything there was to know about the expression and function of mental life. The boy lost faith in himself because his ambition passed from exaggerated heights to nothing—that is to say, to sheer discouragement. Life and school did not fulfill his expectations, and so he turned to law-breaking. By law-breaking he passed out of the control of the educator and the child guidance expert, for society has not yet devised the apparatus for treating criminals, especially juvenile criminals, as educational problems—problems in the correction of psychological mistakes.

There is a curious fact that is familiar to any one who has ever had much to do with pedagogy, and that is the frequency with which we find wayward children in the families of teachers, ministers, doctors and lawyers. This applies not merely to educators without much professional standing but also to those whose opinions we regard as important. Despite their professional authority they seem to be unable to bring about peace and order in their own families. The explanation is that in all such families certain important viewpoints have either been entirely overlooked or not comprehended. Part of the difficulty comes, for instance, from the strict rules and regulations which the educator-parent, by means of his assumed authority, tries to force on his family. He oppresses his children too severely. He threatens their independence and often indeed robs them of it. It seems as if he arouses in them a mood which compels them to take revenge for this oppression, which is rooted in their memory by the rod with which they have been beaten. Also it must be remembered that deliberate pedagogy leads to an extraordinarily sharpened observation. For the most part this is of great advantage, but in the case of one's own children it results often in making the children want to be constantly in the center of attention. They regard themselves as a display experiment, and they look upon the others as the responsible and determining parties. These others have to remove all the difficulties and the children themselves feel free of any responsibility.

CHAPTER FOUR

DIRECTING THE SUPERIORITY STRIVING

W E have seen that every child has a striving for superiority. What a parent or educator has to do is to direct this striving into a fruitful and useful channel. He has to see to it that the striving is productive of mental health and happiness instead of neurosis and disorder.

How is this to be done? What is the basis of differentiating between useful and useless manifestations of the striving for superiority? The answer is, interest in the community. It is impossible to think of any achievement, anything worth while that anybody has ever done, that has no connection with the community. If we recall the great deeds which seem to us noble, lofty and valuable, we shall see that these deeds have been valuable not only to the doer but to the community at large. Hence the education of a child must be so organized that the child will recognize social feeling or a sense of solidarity with the community.

THE EDUCATION OF CHILDREN

Children who do not understand the notion of social feeling become problem children. They are simply children whose striving for superiority has not been turned to use.

It is true that there are wide differences of opinion as to what is useful to the community. One thing, however, is certain: we can judge a tree by its fruits. The results of any particular act will show whether it has been useful or useless to the community. This means that we must take account of time and effects. Eventually the act must intersect with the logic of reality, and this intersection with the logic of reality will show whether the act has any relevance to the needs of the community at large. It is the universal structure of things which is the standard of value, and sooner or later the contradiction or agreement with this standard is bound to come out. It is fortunate, moreover, that in ordinary life we do not find ourselves very often in a situation that requires a complicated technique of judgment. As regards social movements, political trends, etc., whose effect we cannot clearly foresee, there is room for controversy. However, even here—in the life of peoples as well as in individual lives—the effects ultimately indicate whether certain acts are useful and true or not. For from a scientific point of view we cannot call anything good or useful for all unless it is an absolute truth and a correct solution of the problem of life, and the problem of life is conditioned by the earth, the cosmos, and the logic of human inter-relationship. These conditions of the objective and human universe confront us like a mathematical problem which carries its solution within itself, even though we are not always in a position to solve such a problem. We can only decide upon the correctness of the solution when we test it in the light of the data of the problem. It is a pity that sometimes the opportunity to test the truth of a solution comes so late that there is no time to correct mistakes.

Individuals who do not regard their life's structure from a logical and objective point of view are for the most part unable to see the coherence and consistency of their behavior pattern. When a problem presents itself they are appalled, and instead of tackling it they think they have erred in taking a road on which they meet problems. In the case of children it is also to be remembered that when they leave the road of usefulness, they are not in a position to learn positive lessons from negative experiences simply because they do not understand the significance of problems. It is therefore necessary to teach a child to look upon his life, not as a series of unconnected events, but as a continuous thread interpenetrating all the incidents in his existence. No one happening can be taken out from the context of his whole life; it can be explained only in relation to everything that has gone before. When a child understands this he will be able to comprehend why he blundered into the wrong path.

Before discussing further the difference between the right and wrong direction for the striving for superiority, it may be well to take up the kind of behavior which seems to contradict our general theory. This is the behavior of laziness—a type of behavior, which, on the face of it, seems to contradict the view that all children have an innate striving for superiority. In fact the scolding that a lazy child receives is to the effect that he has no striving for superiority, that he has no ambition. But if we examine the situation of the lazy child more closely, we shall see how the ordinary view is mistaken. The lazy child possesses certain advantages. He is not burdened with other people's expectations of himself; he is to a certain extent excused for not accomplishing so much; he does not struggle, and he therefore assumes a negligent, indolent attitude. However, because of his laziness he is often successful in pushing himself into the limelight, since his parents find it necessary to occupy themselves with him. When we consider how many children there are who want to have a position in the foreground at any price, then we can see why some children should hit upon the idea of making themselves noticeable by being lazy.

This, however, is not a complete psychological explanation of laziness. There are many children who adopt a lazy attitude as a means of easing their situation. Their apparent incapacity and their lack of accomplishment are always attributed to laziness. One rarely hears them being accused of incapability; on the contrary their families usually say: "What couldn't he do if he were not lazy?" The children content themselves with the recognition that they *could* accomplish everything if only they were not lazy. This is balm for the ego of the child who has too little confidence in himself. It is a substitute for success, not only in the case of children, but for adults as well. This fallacious if-sentence, "If I were not lazy, what couldn't I do?" quiets their feeling of having failed. When such children really do something, their small deed assumes extra significance in their eyes. The one unimportant accomplishment is something of a contrast to their uniform lack of accomplishment before, and as a result they receive praise for it, while the other children who have always been active receive less recognition for greater accomplishments.

We thus see that there is a hidden and uncomprehended diplomacy in laziness. Lazy children are like tight-rope walkers with a net underneath the rope; when they fall, they fall softly. Criticism of lazy children is milder than of other children, and it insults their ego less. It is less painful to be told that one is lazy than that one is incapable. In short laziness serves as a screen to hide the child's lack of faith in himself, prohibiting him from making attempts to cope with the problems confronting him.

If we consider the current educational methods, we shall see that they exactly meet the wishes of the lazy child. For the more one scolds a lazy child the nearer he is to his goal. One occupies oneself with him all the time, and the scolding diverts attention from the question of his ability, thus fulfilling his desire. Punishment works much the same way. Teachers who think that they can cure a child of laziness by punishing him are always disappointed. The severest punishment cannot make an industrious child out of a lazy one.

If a transformation takes place it is brought

about by a change in the situation, as, for instance, when such a child attains an unexpected success. Or again it may happen when he passes from a strict teacher to a more gentle one, who understands the child, talks with him earnestly and gives him new courage instead of weakening the little courage that he has. In such a situation the change from laziness to activity is sometimes surprisingly sudden. Thus we have the children who are backward in the first years of school and who, on coming to a new school, show themselves unusually industrious because of the change of school environment.

Some children who do not seek escape by means of laziness avoid useful activity by playing sick. Other children are unusually excited at examination time because they have a feeling they will be shown some preference on account of their nervous tension. The same psychological tendency is manifested by children who cry: the crying and the excitement are pleas for privilege.

In the same class with these children are also to be put the children who, on the basis of some defect, demand special consideration—for example the stutterers. Those who have had much to do with tiny children will have noticed that almost all children show a faint tendency to stutter when they begin to speak. The development of speech is, as we know, quickened and retarded by many factors, principally by the degree of social feeling. Children who are socially-minded, who want to make contact with their fellow human beings will learn to speak much more quickly and easily than those who avoid others. There are even situations in which speech is a superfluous activity; for example, in the case of a child so protected and pampered that his every wish is divined and fulfilled before he has time to make his desires known (as is necessarily done with children who are deaf mutes).

When children do not learn to speak before they are four or five the parents begin to be afraid of deaf-mutism. But they soon notice that they are able to hear quite well, which of course excludes the hypothesis of deaf-mutism. On the other hand it is observed that they are really living in an environment in which speech is superfluous. When everything is handed to a child "on a silver platter," as we say, so that he has no urge to speak, then the child will learn to speak very late in life. Speech is an indication of the child's striving for superiority and of the direction of its development. He must speak in order to express his superiority striving, whether this expression takes the form of bringing joy to his family by his utterances or whether it takes the form of helping him attain his ordinary needs. When there is no possibility for this type of expression in either form, then we can naturally expect difficulties in the way of speech development.

There are other speech defects, such as difficulty in the pronunciation of certain consonants, like *r, k* and *s*. They are all curable, and it is therefore rather remarkable that there should be so many adults who stutter, lisp or speak unintelligibly.

Most children grow out of stuttering. A small percentage must be treated. What is involved in the process of treatment may be illustrated from the case of a thirteen-year-old boy. A doctor started to treat this boy when he was six years old. The treatment lasted a year and was unsuccessful. A year followed without professional assistance, then another year with another doctor, the treatment being again unsuccessful. The fourth year nothing was done, and during the first two months of the fifth year he was entrusted to a speech doctor who made his condition worse. Some time later he was sent to an institute specializing in speech defects. The treatment, which lasted two months, was successful, but after a period of six months there was a relapse.

There followed eight months at the hands of still another speech doctor. This time, instead of any improvement being noticed, a gradual deterioration set in. One more doctor was tried but again without success. During the next summer he improved, but at the end of the vacation period he sank back into his old manner of speaking.

Most of the treatment consisted in having the boy read aloud, in slow speaking, exercises, etc. It was remarked that some forms of excitement produced temporary improvement, only to be followed by relapse. The boy had no organic defects, although as a tiny child he had suffered a fall from the second story of a building, which resulted in concussion of the brain.

The boy's teacher, who had known him for a year, described him as "a well-bred, industrious lad who blushes easily and is somewhat irritable." French and geography were the boy's hardest subjects, he said. At examination time he was specially excited. Of his special interests the teacher noted a taste for gymnastics and sports and also a liking for technical work. The boy did not manifest in any way the nature of a leader; he got along well with his schoolmates, but quarrelled occasionally with his younger brother. He was left-handed, and the year before he had had a stroke of facial paralysis on the right side of his face.

Turning to his family environment, we find the father to be a business man, who is very nervous and who often scolds the son severely when he stutters. Despite this the boy has more fear of his mother. He has a tutor at home, and as a result he can seldom leave the house. He rather misses his lack of freedom. He also thinks his mother is unfair because she favors the younger boy.

On the basis of these facts the following explanation may be offered: The boy's ready blushing is an indication of the increase in tension which comes as soon as he must make a social contact. It is, as it were, a relative of his stuttering habit. Even a teacher whom he likes does not succeed in curing him of his stuttering because this stuttering has become mechanized into his system and expresses his general dislike for others.

We know that the motive for stuttering does not lie in the external environment but in the way the stutterer apperceives that environment. His irritability is psychologically very significant. He is not a passive child. His striving for recognition and superiority expresses itself in irritability, as it does with most weak natures. Another proof of his discouragement is revealed by the fact that he quarrels only with a younger boy. His excitement before an examination shows his increased tension due to the fear that he will not be successful and the feeling that he is not as capable as others. He has a strong feeling of inferiority, which diverts his striving for superiority in a useless direction.

Inasmuch as the situation at home is not as agreeable as at school, the boy gladly goes to school. At home the younger brother occupies the center of the stage. It is impossible that an organic wound or fright should have been the cause of his stuttering, but one or the other may have helped rob him of his courage. His younger brother, who has pushed him to one side in the family constellation, has had a greater effect upon him.

It is also significant that the boy suffered from enuresis (bed-wetting) until he was eight years old, a symptom found for the most part only in those children who were first spoiled and pampered and later "dethroned." The bed-wetting is a sure indication that he fought for his mother's attention even at night. It is a sign in this case that the child could not reconcile himself to being left alone.

The boy can be cured through encouragement and through being taught how to be independent. One must put tasks in his way which he can accomplish, and from the accomplishment of which he can gain faith in himself. The boy admits that the arrival of his younger brother was disagreeable to him: he must now be made to understand how his jealousy has driven him into a false turn.

There is much to be said about the symptoms which accompany stuttering. Thus we want to know what happens in a state of excitement. Many stutterers when they become angry can scold without a trace of stuttering showing in their speech. Also older stutterers frequently speak flawlessly when reciting, or when they are in love. These are the facts that indicate that the decisive factor lies in their relation to others. The decisive moment is the confrontation, the tension aroused in the child when he must establish a connection between himself and another, or when he must achieve expression by means of speech.

When a child learns to speak without undue difficulty no one pays much attention to the progress of his speech; but when a child shows difficulties, nothing else is mentioned in the house and the stutterer occupies the center of attention. The family occupies itself exclusively with the child, and the result is of course that the child pays too much attention to his speech. He begins consciously to control his expression, something that children who speak normally do not do. We know that the conscious control of functions which should operate automatically results in a restriction of the function. A pretty example of this is given by Meyrink in his fairy tale, "The Flight of the Toad." The toad meets an animal with a thousand feet and immediately begins praising the powers of this remarkable animal. "Can you tell me," asks the toad, "which one of your thousand legs you move first, and in what order you move the other nine hundred and ninety-nine legs?" The millipede begins to think and starts observing the movements of his legs, and in his attempts to control them he becomes confused and cannot move a single one.

Important as it is to exercise conscious control on the course of our life, it is harmful to attempt to control each individual movement. We are able to produce works of art only when we can automatize the physical movements necessary to produce these works.

Despite the disastrous effect which the stuttering habit has on the future possibilities of the child and despite the obvious disadvantages that accompany the stuttering during the bringing up of the child (the sympathy and the special attention given him by his family), there are still many persons who take refuge in excuses rather than to seek to improve the condition. This applies both to parents and to children, both of whom may have no faith in the future. The child especially is content to lean on others and to maintain an advantage by a seeming disadvantage.

How frequently apparent disadvantages may be turned to advantage is illustrated in one of Balzac's stories. He tells of two tradesmen who tried to get the best of each other in a bargain. While they were thus bargaining one of them began to stutter. The other one noticed, quite surprised, that the stutterer by his stuttering won time enough to think before making his point. He searched quickly for a counter-weapon, and suddenly he made himself unable to hear any more. The stutterer was then at a disadvantage, inasmuch as he had to strain himself in order to make the other one hear. Equality was thereby re-established.

Stutterers should not be handled like criminals even though they sometimes use this mechanism in order to win time for themselves or make others wait. Children who stutter should be encouraged and should be treated gently. Only through friendly enlightenment and through increasing the courage of the child can successful cures be accomplished.

CHAPTER FIVE

THE INFERIORITY COMPLEX

THE striving for superiority and the sense of inferiority go together in every human being. We strive because we feel inferior, and we overcome our feeling of inferiority by successful striving. The sense of inferiority does not, however, become psychologically significant unless either the mechanism of successful striving is obstructed or unless it is increased beyond endurance by the psychological reaction to organ inferiority. Then we have an inferiority complex—an abnormal sentiment of inferiority which necessarily seeks easy compensations and specious satisfactions and which at the same time obstructs the road to successful accomplishment by magnifying the obstacles and decreasing the supply of courage.

Let us consider again in this connection the case of the thirteen-year-old boy who stuttered. His discouragement is, as we have seen, partly responsible for his continued stuttering, and his stuttering increases his discouragement. We thus have here the usual vicious circle of a neurotic inferiority complex. The boy wants to hide himself. He has given up hope; he may even have had thoughts of suicide. The boy's stuttering has become an expression and a continuation of his life's pattern. It makes an impression upon his environment, it puts him in the center of attention, and thus eases his psychological *malaise*.

The boy has set before himself a somewhat overvalued and mistaken goal of counting in the world and amounting to something. He will always strive for prestige, and he must therefore show himself to be good-natured, to be able to get along with others, to have his work in order. On top of that he feels he must have an alibi in case he experiences a defeat, and this alibi is his stuttering. The case of this boy is thus all the more significant because for the most part his life is usefully oriented: it is only in one phase that his judgment and his courage have deteriorated.

Stuttering is of course only one of innumerable weapons which discouraged children use when they do not believe that they will be able to succeed on the strength of their own ability. These weapons of discouragement may be compared to the weapons

which nature has given animals for their protection
—claws and horns. It is easy to see how they have
their origin in the child's weakness, and his despair
of being able to cope with life without such extrane-
ous equipment. And it is remarkable how many
things may serve for such weapons. There are some
children who have no other weapon than their lack
of control of stools and urine. It is an indication that
they do not want to leave their infancy, the state in
which one can live without work and pain. There is
seldom any organic weakness of the intestines or
the bladder in the case of such children. They merely
resort to these things as tricks which will awaken the
sympathy of the parent or educator—and this despite the fact that the same tricks may sometimes
evoke ridicule from their comrades. Such manifestations should therefore not be treated as sicknesses
but as expressions of an inferiority complex, or of
an endangered striving for superiority.

We can visualize how the stuttering complaint
developed, probably out of a very small physiological
core. The boy was an only child for a long time, and
his mother was constantly occupied with him. As he
grew up he probably felt that he was not receiving
enough attention, that his expression was being curtailed, and so he discovered a new trick with which

to draw attention to himself. Stuttering assumed a greater significance: he noticed how the person to whom he spoke watched his mouth. By stuttering he was thus able to secure for himself some of the time and attention that would otherwise have been devoted to the younger brother.

It was not otherwise in school. He found a teacher who devoted much time to him. Thus as a result of his stuttering he was able to assume a role of superiority both at home and at school. He missed none of the popularity which falls to the lot of good students and for which he yearned. He doubtless was a good student, but in any case things were made easier for him.

On the other hand, though his stuttering had the effect of inducing his teacher to be lenient with him, it is scarcely a method to be recommended. The boy is hurt much more than other children when he fails to receive what he considers his quota of attention. This securing of attention became in fact a sore subject with the appearance of the younger brother in the family constellation. Unlike normal children he never developed the ability to spread his interest to others: he made his mother the most important person in his family environment, to the exclusion of everybody else.

THE EDUCATION OF CHILDREN

One must begin the treatment of such children by increasing their courage and by getting them to believe in their own strength and ability. Valuable as it is to establish friendly relations with such children by means of a sympathetic attitude and not to frighten them by stern measures, this is still not enough. The friendly relation must be used to encourage the children to make continued improvement. This can be done only by making the children more independent, by bringing them—through various devices—to the point where they necessarily acquire faith in their own mental and physical powers. They simply must be convinced that what they have not yet achieved can be readily attained by industry, perseverance, practice and courage.

The worst mistake in the education of children is for the parent or educator to prophesy a bad ending for a child who has strayed on the wrong path. Such a stupid prophecy makes the situation infinitely worse since it increases the child's cowardice. One should do just the opposite: inspire the child with optimism. As Virgil said, "they can because they think they can."

It must never be believed that we can influence a child to really improve his conduct by humiliating him or shaming him, even though we sometimes see that children who are afraid of being laughed at seem to change their behavior. How unsound is this stimulation by ridicule may be judged from the following case. There was a boy who was constantly being teased by his friends because he was not able to swim. Finally he could stand the ridicule no longer, and so he jumped from the diving board into deep water. He was saved from drowning only with great difficulty. It may be that a coward who is in danger of losing his prestige does something to counteract his cowardice, but it is seldom the proper act. It is often a cowardly, useless way of meeting his original cowardice, as we see from the case just cited. The real cowardice lay in the fact that the boy was afraid to admit that he could not swim because he would thereby lose standing among his friends. He did not cure that cowardice by desperately jumping into the water, but rather reinforced his cowardly propensity not to face facts.

Cowardice is a trait which always destroys human relations. A child who is always so worried about his own person that he can no longer consider others is willing to achieve prestige at the cost of his fellow human beings. Cowardice thus brings in its wake an individualistic, combative attitude which abolishes social feeling, although it is far from abolishing the fear of others' opinions. A coward is always afraid of being ridiculed by people, of being overlooked, or being degraded. He is thus always at the mercy of of the opinions of others. He is like a person living in an enemy country, and he develops the character traits of suspicion, envy and selfishness.

Children of this cowardly type frequently become critical and nagging persons, reluctant to praise others and resentful if others are praised. It is thus a sign of weakness when one wants to surpass others not through one's own accomplishments but through degrading the others. To rid children of inimical feelings towards others is a pedagogical task which cannot be avoided by those who have recognized the symptoms. He who does not see it is, of course, excused, but he will never know how to correct the resulting unfavorable character traits. But when we know that the problem is to reconcile the child to the world and to life, to show him his mistake and to explain to him that what he wanted was to have the prize of prestige without having worked to achieve it, then we also know in what direction to work upon the child. We know that we have to strengthen the friendly feelings that children should have for one another. We know that we also have to teach children not to look down upon another because he has received a bad mark or because he has done something wrong. Otherwise they build up an inferiority complex and they rob the child of his courage.

When a child is robbed of his faith in the future, the result is that he withdraws from reality and builds up a compensatory striving on the useless side of life. An educator's most important task— one might almost say his holy duty—is to see to it that no child is discouraged at school, and that a child who enters school already discouraged regains his confidence in himself through his school and his teacher. This goes hand in hand with the vocation of the educator, for no education is possible except with children who look hopefully and joyfully upon the future.

There is a type of discouragement which is only temporary, and occurs particularly in the case of ambitious children who, despite the progress they are making, sometimes lose hope because they have passed their last examination and must now turn to the choice of an occupation. Also some ambitious children often give up the fight for a while, when they do not achieve first rank in their examinations. The conflict which unconsciously has been long in preparation suddenly breaks out. It may express itself in complete confusion, or in anxiety neurosis. Such children—if their discouragement is not checked in time—will always be starting something without finishing it; and when they are older they will change their jobs frequently, never believing that anything can end well for them and always fearing defeat.

The self-evaluation of a child is then of the greatest importance. It is impossible, however, to discover what a child really thinks of himself by asking him. No matter how diplomatically we go about it we receive uncertain or indefinite answers. Some children will say that they think rather well of themselves; other children will say that they are worth nothing. Investigation in the latter cases may often disclose that the adults in their environment have said to them hundreds of times, "You aren't worth anything!" or "You are stupid!"

There are few children who can hear so scathing a reproach without being wounded by it. There are others, however, who protect and shield their ego by undervaluing their ability.

If questioning a child does not inform us as to his judgment of himself, we can, however, observe the manner in which he approaches his problem— whether, for example, he goes forward in a confident, decided manner, or whether he exhibits the sign that is to be found most frequently among discouraged children, a hesitating manner. Schematically this may be illustrated by the example of a child who starts to go bravely forward, but who slows down and falters the nearer he approaches his tasks and finally stops altogether at some distance before actual contact with them. Sometimes such children are described as lazy, sometimes as absentminded. The descriptions may be different: the result is always the same. The children do not tackle their work as we expect a normal human being to do, but are always occupied with obstacles. Sometimes a child is so successful in fooling his elders that they fall into the mistake of thinking him lacking in ability. When we keep the whole picture in mind and illuminate it by the principles of Individual Psychology we find that the whole trouble has been the lack of confidence—undervaluation.

When we consider a misdirected striving for superiority we must remember that a completely self-centered individual is an anomaly in society. One often sees children who, because of an inordinate superiority striving, are without consideration for any one else. They are inimical, lawbreaking, greedy and selfish. When they discover a secret they will always use it to hurt some one else.

But in those children whose conduct is most reprehensible we find a trait which is unmistakably human; somewhere or other they have a feeling of belonging to mankind. The relation of their ego to the world around them is implied or expressed in some way although the further their life's scheme is from the conception of co-operation, the more difficult it is to discover any social feeling. We must look for forms of expression which betray the hidden feeling of inferiority. These expressions are innumerable. They begin with the glance of a child. The eye is not only an organ which takes up rays and conducts them further but also an organ for social communication. The way a person looks at another shows the degree of his inclination to connect himself with the other. That is why all psychologists and writers have stressed so much the glance of a human being. We all judge another person's opinion of us by the way he looks at us and we try to discover a part of his soul in his glance. Even though it is possible to make mistakes or to misinterpret, it is somewhat easier to conclude from the glance of a child whether he is a friendly human being.

It is well known that those children who cannot look adults directly in the face open themselves to suspicion. These are not always children with a bad

conscience or children with the habit of sexual malpractice. This glancing away may simply indicate
an attempt to avoid tying himself, however momen-
tarily, to another human being. It indicates the
child's attempt to withdraw from the society of his
comrades. How near a child approaches you when
you call him is also an indication. Many children
remain at some distance, they want to find out first
what it is all about and will approach only when it
is necessary. They regard close contact with suspicion because they have had some bad experiences
and have generalized their one-sided knowledge and
so misused it. It is also interesting to observe the tendency of some children to lean, either on the mother
or on the teacher. The one to whom a child goes more
willingly is much more important than the one whom
he says he loves most.

There are children who reveal a distinct feeling of
confidence and courage in the way they walk, in their
erect carriage and well-carried head, in their firm
voice and lack of timidity. Other children shrink
when they are spoken to and immediately betray
their feeling of inferiority, their fear of not being
able to cope with the situation.

In investigating this inferiority complex we find
many who believe that it is innate. The objection to

this opinion is that any child, no matter how courageous, can be made afraid. A child whose father and mother are timid will probably be timid as well, not because he has inherited the timidity but because he has grown up in an atmosphere permeated with fear. The atmosphere of the family, and the character traits of the parents are most important in the development of a child. Children who keep to themselves in school come more often than not from families having little or no relations with others. It is of course a temptation to think of inherited characteristics in such cases, but this is an exploded theory. No physical changes in the organs or in the brain are able to produce an inability to make contact with others. There are, however, facts which do not necessarily compel such an attitude but which make understandable the appearance of such a peculiarity.

The simplest case which will enable us to understand the matter theoretically is the example of a child born with weak organs, who has been sickly for some time, and oppressed by life because of pain and weakness. Such children are very much occupied with themselves and look upon the outer world as hard and hostile. A second harmful factor plays a role in such cases. A weak child must find a person who makes life easier for him, who devotes himself to the child, and who by this very devotion and protective attitude develops in the child a strong feeling of inferiority. All children, because of the disparity in size and strength between them and adults, have a relative feeling of inferiority. This feeling of being "less" is easily intensified when a child is told, as so frequently happens, "Children should be seen and not heard."

All these impressions sharpen the child's perception of the fact that he is in a disadvantageous position. The realization that he is smaller and less powerful than others is one with which he finds it impossible to reconcile himself. The more the idea that he is smaller and weaker stings him, the greater the efforts that he will make to become more. His striving for recognition has received an added impetus. Instead of trying to arrange his life so that it harmonizes with the lives of those in his immediate surroundings, he creates a new formula, "Think only of yourself." That is a type of child which keeps to himself.

It may be safely stated that the majority of weak, crippled and ugly children have a strong feeling of inferiority, which expresses itself in two extremes. Either they shrink when spoken to, withdraw, are timid, or they are aggressive. Those are two forms of behavior which seem to be totally apart but which may be identified by the same cause. In their striving for recognition such children betray themselves by saying too little one time and too much another. Their social feeling is either ineffectual because they expect nothing from life and believe that they are able to give nothing, or because they subvert the feeling to personal use. They want to be leaders and heroes, always in the center.

When a child has been training himself in a wrong direction for years, it is impossible to expect that a single conversation will change his pattern. The educator must have patience. In such cases where the children make attempts to improve and have an occasional relapse, it is sometimes advisable to explain to the child that improvement does not come quickly. This quiets the child and does not permit him to be discouraged. When a child has been deficient in mathematics for two years he cannot possibly make up the deficiency in two weeks, but that he can make it up is indisputable. A normal child, that is to say, a courageous one, is capable of making up anything. We see again and again that an inability is due to a mistaken development, a peculiar, heavy, graceless formation of the whole personality. It is always possible to help behavior-problem children who are not feeble-minded.

Inability or seeming stupidity, clumsiness, apathy are not sufficient proof of feeble-mindedness. With feeble-minded children there are always physical indications of faulty brain development. This bodily defect may be caused by those glands which affect the development of the brain. Sometimes such physical defects vanish in the course of time, and what remain are only the psychic traces of the original physical deficiency. That is to say, a child who was originally weak because of a weak organism may continue to act as if he were weak even after his body has grown strong.

We must even go further. Not only may psychological inferiority and an egocentric attitude be the result of the past history of organic inferiority and physical weakness, but they may also be brought about by entirely different circumstances that have nothing to do with organic inferiority. They may be brought about through the wrong kind of nourishment, or through a loveless and harsh upbringing. In such cases, life for the child becomes only a misery, and the child assumes a hostile attitude towards his environment. The effects are similar, if not identical, with the disturbance in psychological life resulting from organic inferiority.

We have to expect that we shall have great difficulties in treating those children who have been brought up in an atmosphere devoid of love. They will look upon us as they look upon all others who hurt them; every urge to go to school will be felt as oppression. They will always feel fettered and will always have the tendency to revolt as far as lies in their power. They will not be able to assume a correct attitude towards their comrades because they envy those children who have had a happier childhood.

Such embittered children often develop into characters who like to poison the life of others. They have not been sufficiently courageous to overcome their environment and they try to compensate for their own feeling of lack of power by oppressing those who are weaker, or by being superior to others through an apparent friendliness. This friendliness, however, lasts only as long as the others permit themselves to be dominated. Many children come to the point where they make friends only with those who are in worse circumstances, just as there are adults who feel themselves particularly drawn to sufferers. Or they prefer younger, poorer children. Boys, too, sometimes prefer a particularly gentle, submissive type of girl, without sex entering into their preference.

CHAPTER SIX

THE DEVELOPMENT OF THE CHILD: PREVENTING THE INFERIORITY COMPLEX

W HEN a child takes an unusually long time to learn to walk, but can walk normally once he has learned, it does not mean that the child must develop an inferiority complex for the rest of his life. We know, however, that a child whose mental development is otherwise normal is always strongly impressed by any restriction in the freedom of movement. He feels that his situation is an unhappy one and he is likely to draw pessimistic conclusions from it, which may tend to govern his future course of action, even though the original physical, functional incapacity disappears later. There are many children who at at one time had rickets and who, though cured, still bear the marks of the disease; crooked legs, clumsiness, lung catarrh, a certain malformation of the head (caput quadratum), curved spine, enlarged ankles, feeble joints, bad posture, etc.

What remains psychically is the feeling of defeat which they acquired during their illness, and their consequent inclination to pessimism. Such children see the ease with which their comrades carry on and are oppressed by a feeling of inferiority. They undervalue themselves, and take one of two courses. Either they completely lose confidence and make little if any attempt at progress, or they are spurred on by the seeming desperation of their plight to catch up with their more fortunate playmates in spite of their physical handicap. Children obviously have not sufficient intelligence to be able to judge their situations correctly.

It is a significant fact that what determines the development of the child is neither his own intrinsic ability nor the objective environment, but the interpretation that the child happens to make of the external reality and of his relation to it. The potentialities which a child brings into the world are not of primary importance, nor is our adult judgment of the child's situation of any importance. What is essential is for us to see the child's situation with the eyes of the child himself, and interpret it with his own mistaken judgment. We must not suppose that the child behaves logically —that is to say, according to adult common sense—but we must be ready to recognize that children make mistakes in interpreting their own positions. Indeed, we must remember that the education of children would be impossible were it not for the fact that they make mistakes. We could not possibly educate or improve a child if the mistakes he made were innate. Consequently, he who believes in innate character traits cannot and should not educate children.

It is not true that we always find a healthy mind in a healthy body. It is possible to find a healthy mind in a sick body when a child faces life with courage in spite of physical defects. On the other hand, if a child is physically healthy, but through an untoward set of circumstances has been led to make a fallacious interpretation of his abilities, he will not be mentally healthy. A failure in any given task often makes a child believe in his own incapacity. This is because such children are extraordinarily sensitive to difficulties and regard each obstacle as a confirmation of their lack of power.

Some children in addition to having difficulties in motor activities find it hard to learn to speak. Learning to speak should usually accompany learning to walk. The two are of course not actually connected but are dependent upon the rearing of the child and the circumstances of the family. Some children who would otherwise have no difficulty fail to speak because the family neglects to help them. It is clear, however, that any child who is not deaf and whose speech organs are otherwise perfect should learn to speak at a reasonably early age. Under certain circumstances, especially in extremely visual types, speech is delayed. In other cases, parents spoil the child by saying everything for him instead of letting him make the attempt to express himself. Such a child takes so long to learn to speak that we sometimes think he is deaf. When he finally does learn to speak, his interest in speaking has become so intensified that he frequently becomes an orator in later life. Klara Schumann, the wife of the composer, could not speak until she was four and could speak only a little even when she was eight. She was a peculiar child, very reserved, and she preferred to spend her time idling in the kitchen. We can deduce from this that no one bothered her. "Peculiar," said her father, "that this striking mental discord was the beginning of a life so full of wonderful harmony." Hers is an example of an over-compensation.

THE EDUCATION OF CHILDREN

One must be careful to see that children who are deaf and dumb receive special schooling, because it appears to be more and more the fact that complete deafness happens infrequently. No matter how defective a child's hearing is, his little ability to hear should be nursed to the utmost. Professor Katz, in Rostock, has demonstrated that he has been able to train children who were considered unmusical to a full appreciation of music and the beauty of sound.

Sometimes children who are successful in most of their school subjects fail terribly in one, frequently in mathematics, thereby arousing the suspicion of a light form of imbecility. It is always possible that children who are not successful in arithmetic have at one time or another been frightened by the subject and discouraged in their attempts to cope with it. There are families, occasionally among artists, who boast of the fact that they cannot calculate. In addition, the general idea that mathematics is harder for girls than for boys is wrong. There are many women who are excellent mathematicians and expert statisticians. Schoolgirls often hear "boys can count better than girls" and are discouraged by the remark.

It is an important indication whether a child

can use figures or not. Mathematics is one of the few fields of knowledge which gives a human being security. It is a thought-operation which leads to the stabilization of surrounding chaos by numbers. People with a strong feeling of insecurity are usually bad calculators.

This is true of other subjects too. Writing, the affixing to paper of the sounds known only to inner consciousness, gives security to the individual. Drawing permits making permanent a fleeting optical impression. Gymnastics and dancing are expressions of attainment to physical security and, more especially, by virtue of the sure control of our bodies, of a modicum of mental security. Probably this is why so many educators are such firm believers in sports.

A striking manifestation of a feeling of inferiority in children is the difficulty in learning to swim. When a child learns to swim easily, it is a good sign that he will also be able to overcome other difficulties. A child who finds it hard to learn to swim shows lack of faith in himself and in his swimming instructor. It is noteworthy that many children who have difficulty at first, become excellent swimmers later on. These are the children who, sensitive to the original difficulty, have been spurred on by eventual success to a goal of perfection and who frequently become champion swimmers.

It is important to know whether a child is particularly attached to one person or is interested in several. Usually, a child is attached most deeply to his mother, or, failing her, to another member of the family. This ability to attach himself is present in every child unless he is an imbecile or an idiot. When a child has been reared by his mother and attaches himself to another person in the family, it is important to discover why. Obviously, no child should concentrate all his affection and attention on his mother, for a mother's most important function is to spread the interest and confidence of the child to his fellowmen. Grandparents also play an important role in the development of a child—usually a pampering role. The reason for it is that aging people are afraid that they are no longer necessary. They develop exaggerated inferiority feelings and as a result assume the role of nagging critics or of soft-hearted, good-natured elders who, in order to make themselves important to the children, deny them nothing. Children when visiting grandparents are often so spoiled that they refuse to return to their more disciplined homes. Upon their return they complain that it is not as nice at home as it is at their grandparents'. We mention here the role that grandparents sometimes play in the lives of children so that educators will not overlook this important fact in investigating the style of life of any particular child.

Clumsiness in movement (Question Two of the Psychological Questionnaire *) resulting from rickets and remaining unimproved over a long period, usually points to the fact that the child received too much care and was therefore pampered. Mothers should have enough intelligence not to kill a child's independence even when the child is ill and needs special attention.

An important question is whether the child has given much trouble (Question Three). When we hear that this has been the case we can be sure that the mother has been too closely attached to the child. She has not been successful in establishing independence in him. This trouble-making usually manifests itself when going to sleep or getting up, in eating and washing, also in nightmares, or enuresis (bed-wetting). All these symptoms point

---

* See Appendix I.

to an attempt to get the attention of a certain person. One symptom after another appears; it is as if the child were discovering one weapon after another to use in his fight to dominate the older person. We may be sure that when a child develops such symptoms his environment is weak. Punishment does not help, and such children usually tease their parents into punishing them in order to show them that this punishment is of no avail.

An especially important question concerns the development of the intelligence of the child. This is sometimes difficult to answer correctly and it is occasionally advisable to resort to Binet tests, which, however, do not always give reliable results. This is true of all other intelligence tests which should never be accepted as constant for the entire life of the child. In general, the development of intelligence depends a great deal upon family circumstances. Families in better circumstances are able to help their children, and children with good physical development usually show a comparatively good mental development. Unfortunately, it is also so arranged that those children who progress more smoothly in their mental growth are predetermined to the "quality work," or better jobs; while those who grow more slowly are assigned to menial work. As far as we have been able to observe, the system newly introduced in many countries of having special classes for weaker children works out so that most of these children come from poor families. The conclusion to be drawn is that these poorer children, had they been surrounded by more favorable environment, would undoubtedly have been able to compete successfully with children lucky enough to be born into families of better material circumstances.

Another important point to be investigated is whether the child has ever been the butt of ridicule or discouraged by teasing. Some children can bear such discouragement; others lose courage, avoid the difficult roads of useful work, and turn their attention to outward appearances, an indication that a child has little faith in himself. An indication of a hostile environment is to be found when a child is constantly quarreling with others, afraid that if he is not the aggressor the others will attack first. Such children are disobedient; they believe obedience to be a sign of subordination. They think that the courteous return of a greeting is a degradation, they answer impertinently; they never complain because they regard the sympathy of others as a personal humiliation. They never cry in front of others, and sometimes laugh when they should cry, which looks like a lack of feeling, but is only an indication of a fear of showing weakness. No act of cruelty has ever been done which has not been based upon a secret weakness. The person who is really strong has no feeling for cruelty. Such disobedient children are often dirty, personally negligent, bite their nails and pick their noses, and are very stubborn. They need to be encouraged and it must be made clear to them that their actions only indicate their fear of appearing as weaklings.

Question Four, namely, whether the child makes friends easily or is unfriendly, whether he is a leader or a follower, has to do with his ability to make contacts—that is to say, with his degree of social feeling or discouragement. It also has to do with his desire to obey or to rule. When a child isolates himself, he indicates that he has not sufficient confidence in himself to compete with others, and that his striving for superiority is so strong that he fears the subordination of his personality in the crowd. Children having a tendency to collect things indicate that they want to strengthen themselves and surpass others. This tendency to collect is dangerous because it can very easily go too far and develop into inordinate ambition or greed, the expression of a general feeling of weakness which seeks a point of support. Such children are easily led to steal when they believe that they have been neglected or overlooked, because they feel this lack of attention more than others.

Question Five concerns the child's attitude to school. We must notice whether he is tardy and whether he is excited about going to school (such excitement frequently being an indication of reluctance). The fears the children have in the face of certain situations are variously expressed. When they have homework to do, they become irritable; they have what seems like a heart palpitation caused by the tense state into which they work themselves. One type in particular may have certain organic changes, such as sexual excitement. The system of giving children marks is not always a commendable one. Children would be relieved of a great burden if they were not classified in such a way. School becomes a sort of constant examination or test in which a good mark is necessary to strive for, while a bad mark is like a permanent judgment.

Does the child do his homework willingly, or

must he be forced to do it? To forget to do one's homework shows the tendency to avoid responsibility. Unsatisfactory school work and impatience with it are sometimes means used for escaping school, because the child wants to do something else.

Is the child lazy? When a child fails in school work, he prefers to have laziness as the reason rather than inability. When a lazy child performs one task well, he is praised, and then he hears, "He could accomplish so much if he were not lazy." The child is satisfied with this opinion because he is convinced that he no longer has to prove his ability. To this type belong also the indolent children who lack courage, who cannot concentrate, who are always dependent; pampered children who disturb classroom work because they want to draw attention to themselves.

The question, What is the child's attitude toward his teacher? is not an easy one to answer. Children usually mask their real feelings toward their teachers. When a child constantly criticizes, and tries to humiliate his school friends, we may assume that this tendency to degrade is an indication of his own lack of faith in himself. Such children are arrogant, nagging, always know everything better than the others. This attitude masks their own weakness.

Children more difficult to handle are the indifferent, apathetic, passive ones. They also wear a mask since they are not really so indifferent. When such children are driven beyond control, their reaction generally takes the form of a fit of furious passion or an attempt at suicide. They never do anything until they are ordered to do so. They are afraid of setbacks and overvalue other persons. They must be encouraged.

Children who show themselves ambitious in sport or gymnastics betray the fact that they have been ambitious in other directions, but have been afraid of defeat. Children who read far more than is customary lack courage and indicate that they hope to win power through reading. Such children have a rich imaginative life but are timid in facing reality. It is also important to note what kind of stories children prefer: novels, fairy tales, biographies, travel or objective, scientific works. During puberty children are easily attracted to pornographic books. It is unfortunate that in every large city there are bookstores that make a practice of selling such printed matter. The increased sexual drive and the longing for experience turn their thoughts in this direction. The following means are to be employed in combatting such harmful influences: preparation of children for their role as fellow men, sexual clarification at an early age and friendly relations with their parents.

Question Six concerns family conditions—sickness in the family, such as alcoholism, neuroses, tuberculosis, lues (syphilis), epilepsy. It is also important to have a comprehensive physical history of the child. A child who breathes through his mouth frequently has a stupid facial expression, resulting from adenoids and tonsils which prevent correct breathing. An operation to remove such obstructions is important, and sometimes the belief that the operation is going to help him gives the child more courage to tackle school upon his return.

Sickness in the family frequently harms the progress of a child. Parents who are chronically ill burden their children heavily. Nervous and psychic disorders oppress the whole family. Whenever it is possible, children should not be permitted to know that a member of the family has become mentally afflicted. A mental disorder casts a shadow over the whole family apart from the superstition that it can be inherited. This is also true of the innumerable cases of tuberculosis and cancer. All such diseases make a horrible impression on the mind of a child and it is sometimes much better to take the child out of such a home atmosphere. Chronic alcoholism or criminal inclinations within a family act like a poison which the child is frequently unable to resist. However, there are difficulties in the way of the proper placement of children taken from such homes. Epileptics are usually irritable and disturb the harmony of family life. But what is worst of all is syphilis. Children of syphilitic parents are usually very weak, inherit the disease and find it tragically hard to cope with life.

We cannot overlook the fact that the material conditions of the family color the child's outlook on life. Poverty in comparison with the better circumstances of other children arouses a feeling of insufficiency. Children who are moderately well-off find it difficult to go without their customary comforts if the family's finances decline. The tension is still greater when grandparents are better off than the parents, as in the case of Peter Ghent, who could not rid himself of the thought that his grandfather was extremely powerful while his father failed in everything. A child often becomes industrious as a protest against an indolent father.

The first contact with death when it comes suddenly is frequently a shock great enough to influence the whole life of the child. A child who is unprepared for death and is suddenly brought face to face with it, realizes for the first time that life has an end. This may discourage the child completely, or at least make him very timid. In the biographies of doctors we often find that their choice of a profession was caused by a brusque meeting with death, a proof that a child is deeply affected by his realization of death. It is not advisable to burden children with this problem because they are not able to comprehend it entirely. Orphans or step-children often blame their unhappiness on the death of their parents.

It is important to know who has the deciding voice in the family. Usually it is the father. When a mother or a step-mother dominates, the results are abnormal, and the father frequently loses the respect of his children. Sons of dominating mothers usually carry with them a certain fear of women of which they rarely can rid themselves. Such men either avoid women or make life unpleasant for the women in their families.

It is further necessary to know whether the child's rearing has been strict or mild. Individual Psychologists do not believe that either severe or mild methods should be used in rearing children. What is necessary is understanding, avoidance of mistakes and constant encouragement of the child to face and solve his problems and develop social feeling. Parents who nag their children harm them, for they discourage the children completely. A pampering education develops a dependent attitude and a tendency to cling to one person. Parents should avoid both the painting of rosy pictures and the describing of the world in pessimistic terms. Their job is to give the child as good a preparation for life as possible, so that the child will be able to take care of himself. Children who have not been taught how to face difficulties will seek to avoid every hardship, which leads to an ever-narrowing circle of activity.

It is important to know who has charge of the children. It is not necessary that a mother be constantly with her children, but she must know the person in whose care she places them. The best way to teach a child is to let him learn from experience, within reason, so that his conduct is guided not by the restrictions placed upon him by others but by the logic of facts.

Question Seven concerns the position of the child in the family constellation, which is most suggestive of the child's character. An only child is in a peculiar situation; a youngest child, an only boy among girls or an only girl among boys, are also in peculiar positions.

Question Eight concerns the choice of an occupation. This is an important question because it reveals to us the influence of the environment, the amount of the child's courage and social feeling, and the life rhythm of the child. Day-dreams (question nine) are also significant, as well as early childhood remembrances (question ten). Those people who have learned to interpret childhood remembrances can frequently discover from them the entire style of life. Dreams are also an indication of the direction in which a child is going, an indication of whether he is attempting to solve or to evade his problem. It is important to know whether a child has speech defects; further, whether he is ugly or good-looking, well-formed or badly-formed (question thirteen).

Question Fourteen. Will the child discuss his

situation openly or not? Some children are given to boasting as a compensation for their feeling of inferiority. Others refuse to talk, fearing that they will be taken advantage of, or fearing a new hurt if they betray their weakness.

Question Fifteen. A child who is successful in one subject, say in drawing or music, must be encouraged on the basis of this to improve in his other subjects.

Children who at the age of fifteen do not know what they want to become, are to be regarded as completely discouraged and must be treated accordingly. The occupation of the members of the family as well as the social differences in rank between the brothers and sisters, must be considered. The whole development of a child can be harmed by the unhappy marriage of the parents. It is the duty of the teacher to proceed with prudence, to form a correct picture of the child and his environment, and to arrange his treatment and his attempts to improve the child in accordance with the knowledge gained from the questionnaire.

CHAPTER SEVEN

SOCIAL FEELING AND THE OBSTACLES
TO ITS DEVELOPMENT

I N contrast to the cases of superiority striving we have discussed in the previous chapters, there is to be found a tendency among many children and adults to unite themselves with other human beings, to accomplish their tasks in co-operation with others and to make themselves generally useful from a social point of view. Such manifestations may best be described by the term social feeling. What is the root of this feeling? This is a matter of some controversy. But so far as the present writer has been able to discover, it seems that we have to do here with a phenomenon that is indissolubly connected with the very notion of man.

One may perhaps ask in what sense such a psychological sentiment is more innate than the psychological striving for superiority. The answer would be that both at bottom have the same core—that the individualistic desire for supremacy and the feeling of social-mindedness rest on the same basis in human nature. They both are expressions of a root desire for affirmation; they differ in their form, and their different forms involve different implicit judgments about human nature. Thus the individualistic striving for supremacy involves a judgment that the individual can do without the group, while the feeling of social-mindedness involves the view of a certain dependence upon the group. As views on human nature, there is no doubt that the social feeling is superior to the individualistic striving. The former represents a sounder and logically more fundamental outlook, while the latter is only a superficial viewpoint even though as a psychological phenomenon it is more often to be met with in the lives of individuals.

If we want to see in what sense the social feeling has truth and logic on its side we have only to observe man historically, and we shall notice that man has always lived in groups. Nor is this fact astonishing when we reflect further that those creatures who individually are not able to protect themselves have been compelled always to live together for self-preservation. We have only to compare a human being with a lion to realize that man, regarded as a species of animal, is quite insecure, and that most other animals comparable in size to man are stronger and better armed by nature for physical offense and defense. Darwin observed that all animals whose defense equipment has been somewhat neglected by nature always travel in packs. The orang-utan, for example, with his extraordinary bodily strength, lives alone with his mate, while the smaller and weaker members of the ape family are always to be found in groups. The formation of groups serves, as Darwin has pointed out, as a substitute or compensation for that which nature has denied to the animals individually—claws, fangs, wings, etc.

The formation of groups not only balances what the particular animals lack as individuals, but it also leads them to discover new methods of protection which improve their situation. There are groups of monkeys, for instance, who know how to send out advance scouts to discover the presence of enemies. In this way they are able to bring to bear their massed strength so as to more than make up for the weakness of each member of the group.

We also find a buffalo herd massing itself together and thus defending the group successfully against individual enemies of far greater power.

Animal sociologists who have studied this problem also report that in these groups we often find arrangements which are the equivalent of laws. Thus the scouts that are sent ahead must live according to certain rules, and every blunder or infraction is punished by the whole herd.

It is interesting to note in this connection that many historians assert that the oldest laws of mankind were those which affected the watchmen of the tribe. If this is so, we have a picture of the invention of the group idea out of the inability of weaker forms of animal life to protect themselves. And in a certain sense the feeling of social-mindedness is always a reflection of physical weakness and is inseparable from it. Thus in the case of human beings perhaps the most important situation that fosters social feeling is the helplessness and slow development of infants and children.

In the whole realm of animal life we find no being except man whose young come into the world with such complete helplessness. Also, as we know, the human child requires the longest time to reach maturity. This is not because of the infinite number of things a child must learn before he becomes an adult, but because of the way he develops. Children need the protection of the parents much longer because their organism demands it, and the human race would die out if children were not afforded such protection. The physical weakness of the child may be taken as the occasion which links together education and social-mindedness. Education is a necessity because of the child's physical immaturity, and the goal of education is provided by the fact that the overcoming of the child's immaturity can only be had by relying on the group. Education must necessarily be social in purpose.

In all our rules and methods for the education of children we must always have the idea of community life and social adjustment to it. Whether we know it or not we are always impressed more favorably by that which is good from the standpoint of the community, and less favorably by an act which is generally disadvantageous or harmful to society.

All educational mistakes which we observe are mistakes only because we judge that they will produce harmful effects on the community. All great accomplishments, and in fact all development of a

119

human being's abilities take place under the pressure of social life and in the direction of social feeling.

Let us take, for example, speech. A human being living alone needs no knowledge of speech. That human beings have developed speech is an indisputable indication of the necessity for communal life. Speech is a distinct bond between people and at the same time a product of their living together. The psychology of speech is conceivable only when we use as a point of departure the idea of the community. Individuals living alone have no interest in speech. Whenever a child lacks this broad base of participation in the community and grows up isolated, his ability to speak will be retarded. What we call a talent for speaking can only be acquired and improved when one individual attaches himself to others.

It has been commonly assumed that those children who can express themselves better than others are simply more talented. This is not true. Those children who find difficulty in speaking or in making contact through speech usually do not have strong social feeling. Children who do not learn to speak well are frequently spoiled children, for whom their mothers do everything before the children have time to ask for anything. In this way they lose contact and the ability for social adjustment because they do not need speech.

There are also some children who are reluctant to speak because their parents never permit them to finish a sentence or to answer for themselves; others have been laughed at or ridiculed, and thereby discouraged. This constant correcting and nagging seems to be a widely spread malpractice in the education of children. The dire result is that such children carry with them for years a feeling of degradation and inferiority. One can notice it in such persons who use the stereotyped introduction before they begin a sentence: "But, please don't laugh at me." We hear this frequently and we recognize at once that such people were laughed at frequently when they were children.

There is the case of a child who could speak and hear but whose parents were both deaf and dumb. He always cried without making any sound when he hurt himself. It was necessary to let his parents see the pain, but useless to make his suffering audible.

The development of other abilities of human beings, for example, the growth of understanding or of a logical sense, is unthinkable without social feeling. A man living absolutely alone has no need of logic, or at least has no more need than any other animal. On the other hand, a man who is always in contact with others, who must use speech and logic and common sense in his dealings with others, must develop or acquire social feeling. This is the final goal of all logical thought.

Occasionally the actions of people appear stupid to us when in reality these actions are quite intelligent in the light of their personal goals. This frequently happens with those people who think that everybody else must think as they do, which shows us how significant the factor of social feeling or common sense is in judgment (not to mention that the development of common sense would not be necessary if communal life were not so complicated and did not present the individual with so many intricate problems). We can very well imagine that primitive people have remained at a primitive level because the relative simplicity of their existence did not stimulate them to deeper thought.

Social feeling plays a most important part in the ability of human beings to speak and to think logically—two functions which we might almost regard as holy. If everyone attempted to solve his problems regardless of the community in which he lived, or to use a language of his own, chaos would result. Social feeling gives a security which each individual can feel and which is for him the main support in life. It may not be completely identical with the confidence that we derive from logical thought and truth, but it is the most palpable component of that confidence. To take an illustration, why are calculating and counting so confidently accepted on all sides so that we tend to regard as precisely true only that which we can express in numbers? The reason is that number operations are more easily communicable to our fellow men, at the same time that they are easier for the mind to work with. We do not have much confidence in truths which we cannot communicate to others and have others share with us. This train of thought was doubtless behind Plato's attempt to model all philosophy on number and mathematics. We see the connection with social feeling even more closely from the fact that he wanted the philosopher to go back to the "cave," that is to say, to participate in the life of his fellow men. Even the philosopher, he felt, could not live properly without the security that comes from social feeling.

Children who have, so to speak, less of an accumulation of this feeling of security, reveal it when they come in contact with others or when they have to perform certain tasks on their own initiative. They reveal it particularly in school in those subjects which require objective, logical thinking, as in mathematics.

The conceptions for which a human being is prepared in childhood (for example, moral feelings, ethics, etc.) are usually presented in a one-sided manner. An ethics for a human being who is condemned to live alone is inconceivable. Morals are only in place when we think of the community and the rights of others. This view is a little more difficult to confirm when we think of æsthetic feelings, of our inclination to artistic creations. However, even in the realm of art we can perceive a generally consistent impression which probably has its basic roots in an understanding of health, strength, correct social development, etc. So far as art is concerned the boundaries are elastic, and there is perhaps more room for individual taste. On the whole, however, even æsthetics follows social lines.

If the practical question is put to us—how can we tell the degree to which social feeling has been developed in a child?—we must answer that there are certain conduct manifestations to be considered. When we see, for example, that children, in their striving for superiority, force themselves to the front with no consideration for others, we may be sure that they have less social feeling than those children who avoid that particular procedure. It is impossible to imagine a child in our present civilization without some desire for individualistic supremacy. As a result, his degree of social feeling is usually not sufficiently developed. This is the condition which the critics of mankind, the old and modern moralists have always complained of —that man is by nature egotistical and thinks more of himself than he does of others. This has always been expressed in the form of a sermon which has no effect on children or adults, because nothing can be accomplished with this axiom alone, and people have eventually consoled themselves by thinking that everybody else is no better.

When we deal with children whose ideas have become so confused that they have developed harmful or criminal tendencies, we must recognize that no amount of moral preaching has ever had any effect. In such a situation it is much more desirable to probe a little deeper in order to be able to abolish the evil by pulling up the roots. In other words, we must relinquish our role of judge and assume that of comrade or doctor.

If we constantly tell a child that he is bad or stupid, he will become convinced in a short time that we are right and he will not have sufficient courage thereafter to tackle any task presented to him. What happens then is that the child fails in whatever he tries to do. The belief that he is stupid takes firmer root. He does not understand that the environment originally destroyed his self-confidence and that he is subconsciously arranging his life to prove this fallacious judgment correct. The child feels himself less able than his comrades, he feels himself restricted in abilities and possibilities. His attitude shows unmistakably his depressed frame of mind, which is in direct proportion to the amount of pressure exerted upon him by an unfavorable environment.

Individual Psychology has tried to show that the influence of the environment is always perceptible in every mistake made by a child; for example, a disorderly child is always in the shadow of a person who puts his things in order; a child who lies is always under the influence of a domineering adult who wants to cure the child of lying by harsh means. We can even detect traces of the environment in a child's boasting. Such a child usually feels that praise is a necessity, and not the successful accomplishment of any given task; and in his striving for superiority he is constantly seeking to evoke laudatory comments from the members of his family.

There are situations in the life of every child which parents have usually overlooked or misunderstood. Thus, each child in a family of brothers and sisters is in a different situation. The first child has the unique position of having been for a while the only child. This experience is unknown to a second-born. The youngest child experiences a set of circumstances which not every child goes through, because he remains for a while the smallest and weakest in the environment. There are variations of these situations. When two brothers or two sisters grow up together, the one who is naturally older and more competent has overcome certain difficulties which the younger has still to conquer. The younger of two such children is in a relatively unfavorable position and feels it. To compensate for this feeling of inferiority, the child may increase his striving so as to overtake the older brother or sister.

THE EDUCATION OF CHILDREN

Individual psychologists who have worked for a long time with children are usually able to detect the position that children have had in the family constellation. When the older child is one that has made normal progress, the younger one has been stimulated to greater effort to keep up with the older. As a result the younger is usually more active and more aggressive. If the older child has been weak and has developed slowly, the younger is not forced to make quite so strong an effort in competition.

It is, therefore, important to determine what position a child has had in the family since a child can be completely understood only when his place in the family constellation has been discovered. The youngest children in families bear unmistakable signs of the fact that they have been the youngest. Of course there are exceptions but the most common type of the youngest child is the one who wants to surpass all the others, the one who is never quiet, who is always stirred to further action by the feeling and belief that he must eventually amount to more than all the others. These observations are significant for the education of children because they condition the adoption of certain educational methods. It is impossible to follow the same rules in handling all children. Each child is unique, and while we classify children according to certain general types, we must be careful to treat each child as an individual. This is a condition almost impossible to fulfill in the school, but certainly one obtainable at home.

The youngest child belongs to the type which always wants to be in the foreground of any picture and in many cases he is successful. This is an extraordinarily important consideration since it weakens considerably the notion of the inheritance of mental characteristics. When youngest children of different families bear so much resemblance to each other there is not much room for the belief in inheritance.

Another type of youngest child, directly opposite to the active one described above, is the completely discouraged adolescent. Such a child is as indolent as possible. We can understand that the seemingly great difference between these two types is explainable psychologically. No one is so easily hurt by difficulties as he who has the inordinate ambition to excel all others. His ambition makes him unhappy, and when the obstacles seem almost insurmountable he takes to flight more quickly than one whose striving does not have such an important goal. We see in these two types of youngest child the personification of the Latin saying "Aut Cæsar, aut nullus" or, as we say, "all or nothing."

In the Bible we can find excellent descriptions of youngest children which coincide exactly with our experience—for example, the stories of Joseph, David, Saul, etc. The objection that may be raised that Joseph had a younger brother, Benjamin, may be refuted by the fact that Benjamin was born when Joseph was seventeen years old, so that Joseph as a child was the youngest. How often do we see in life families supported by the youngest child. We find confirmation for our assertion concerning the youngest child not only in the Bible but also in fairy tales. There is no fairy tale in which the youngest child does not surpass all his brothers and sisters—in German, Russian, Scandinavian or Chinese fairy tales the youngest is always the conqueror. It is impossible that this should be only coincidence. It is probably caused by the fact that in former days the figure of the youngest child was much more salient than it is to-day. This type must have been better observed because it was probably easier to notice under primitive conditions.

Much more could be written about the characteristics which children develop in accordance with their position in the family constellation. Oldest children also have many characteristics in common and may be divided into two or three main types.

The present writer had been studying the matter for a long time and the subject was not quite clear in his mind when he accidentally stumbled upon a passage in Fontane's autobiography. Fontane describes there how his father, a French emigrant, took part in a war of Poland against Russia. His father was always very happy when he read, for example, that ten thousand Poles had beaten fifty thousand Russians and put them to flight. Fontane could not understand his father's joy. On the contrary, he objected very much on the ground that fifty thousand Russians simply had to be stronger than ten thousand Poles, and "if that isn't so, it doesn't please me at all because the stronger should always remain the stronger." In reading this paragraph we immediately jump to the conclusion, "Fontane is an oldest child!" Only an oldest child could make such a statement. He remembers his possession of power in the family when he was the only child and feels it an injustice to be dethroned by a weaker person. As a matter of fact it has been found that oldest children usually have a conservative trait. They are believers in power, in rule, and in unbreakable laws. They have a tendency to accept despotism quite frankly and without apology. They have the right attitude for positions of power because they have once occupied such positions themselves.

There are exceptions, as we have said, in the types of oldest children. There is one exception which should be mentioned here. It concerns a problem in child life which has hitherto been neglected. This is the tragic role which an older boy plays when he has a younger sister. Descriptions of confused, completely discouraged boys have very often indicated, without the fact itself being mentioned, that the trouble was a younger, clever sister. The frequency with which this occurs is not an accident because there is a natural explanation for it. We know that in our present civilization men are considered of more importance than women. A first-born son is frequently pampered. His parents expect a great deal of him. His situation is a favorable one until a sister suddenly appears. The girl enters an environment which contains a spoiled older brother who regards her as an annoying intruder and who fights against her.

This situation spurs the girl on to make extraordinary efforts, and if she does not break down, this stimulation affects her whole life. The girl develops rapidly and frightens the older boy, who suddenly sees the fiction of masculine superiority destroyed. He becomes uncertain, and since nature has so arranged matters that girls between the ages of fourteen and sixteen develop mentally and physically more rapidly than boys, his uncertainty is likely to end in a complete defeat. He easily loses his belief in himself and gives up the fight, arranges plausible excuses, or puts difficulties in his own way which he can then use as alibis for ceasing to struggle.

There is a great number of such first-born boys who are confused, hopeless, inexplicably lazy, or suffering from nervousness for no other reason than that they did not feel strong enough to compete with a younger sister. Such boys are sometimes possessed of an unbelievable hatred of the female sex. Their fate is usually a sad one because there are few people who understand their condition and can explain it to them. Sometimes it goes so far that parents and other members of the family complain, "Why isn't it the other way around? Why isn't the boy a girl, and the girl a boy?"

Boys who are alone among several sisters also have characteristics in common. It is difficult to prevent a dominantly feminine atmosphere in a house where there are several girls and only one boy. It either happens that he is very much spoiled by all the members of the family, or that all the women exclude him. Such boys naturally develop differently, but certain traits are common to all of them. We know that the conception that boys should not be educated by women exclusively is very widespread. That is not to be taken literally, since all boys are first reared by women. But what is really meant is that boys should not be brought up in an environment of women. This is not an argument against femininity but against the misunderstandings which arise out of such a situation. It also holds good for a girl who grows up with boys. The boys usually look down upon the girl and she tries, as a result, to imitate the boys in order to be their equal, which is an unfortunate preparation for her later life.

No matter how tolerant one is, it is impossible to join in the chorus of those who believe that girls should be brought up like boys. One can do it for a while but certain unavoidable differences make themselves quickly apparent. Men have different roles to play in life determined by their difference in physical structure. This plays a part in the choice of a profession and girls who are not satisfied with their feminine role sometimes find great difficulty in adjusting themselves to the occupations open to them. When we come to the question of preparation for marriage, it is clear that the education for the role of a woman must be different from that for the part of a man. Girls who are dissatisfied with their sex will object to marriage as a personal degradation or if they do marry they will try to rule. Boys who have been brought up like girls will also experience great difficulty in adjusting themselves to our present form of civilization.

We must not forget in considering all this that a child's style of life is usually determined by the time he is four or five years old. Those are the years during which he must develop social feeling and the flexibility necessary for adjustment. By the time a child is five years old his attitude to his environment is usually so fixed and mechanized that it proceeds in more or less the same direction for the rest of his life. His apperception of the outer world remains the same; the child is caught in the trap of his perspectives and repeats unceasingly his original mental mechanisms and the resulting actions. Social feeling is limited by the boundaries of the individual's mental horizon.

CHAPTER EIGHT

THE CHILD'S POSITION IN THE FAMILY: THE PSYCHOLOGY OF THE SITUATION AND THE REMEDY

W E have seen that children develop in accordance with their unconscious interpretation of the position they occupy in relation to their environment. We have also seen that first, second and third children develop differently, each in accordance with his particular position in the family constellation. This early condition may be regarded as a test of the character developed by the child.

The education of a child cannot begin too soon. As a child grows he develops a certain set of rules or formulas which regulate his conduct and determine his reactions to various situations. When a child is very young there are only slight indications of the particular mechanism he is constructing to guide his future behavior. Later on, as the result of years of training, this behavior pattern becomes fixed and he no longer reacts objectively but in accordance with his unconscious interpretation of the sum total of his past experiences. When a child has made a false interpretation of any particular situation or of his own ability to cope with a particular difficulty, this erroneous judgment will determine his conduct and no amount of logic or common sense can change the adult conduct until the original, childish misinterpretation is corrected.

There is always something subjective in the development of a child and it is this individuality which pedagogues must investigate. It is this individuality which prevents the application of general rules in the education of groups of children. This is also the reason why the application of the same rule results differently with different children.

On the other hand when we see children reacting to the same situation in almost the same way we cannot say that this is because of a law of nature; what is true is that human beings are prone to make the same mistakes because of their common lack of understanding. It is customarily believed that a child always becomes jealous when another child appears in the family. One objection to this generalization is that there are exceptions; another, that a knowledge of how to prepare children for the arrival of a younger brother or sister would make jealousy impossible. A child who makes a mistake may be compared to a person who finds himself in the mountains in front of a footpath. He does not know where or how to proceed. When he has finally found the right path and has come to the next town, he hears people say in astonishment: "Almost everyone who wanders off that path gets lost." Mistakes made by children are often along such enticing paths. They look easy to tread, and thus attract the child.

There are many other situations which have immeasurable influences upon the character of a child. How often do we see two children in a family, one who is good and one who is bad? If we investigate the circumstances a little more closely, we find that the bad child has an intense desire for superiority, wants to dominate all the others and uses all his power to rule the environment. The house is noisy with his cries. The other child, by way of contrast, is quiet, modest, the family's favorite, and held forth as an example to the other. The parents do not know how to explain such opposites in the same family. Upon examination we see that the good child has discovered that he is able to gain much more recognition by his excellent behavior and competes successfully with his bad brother or sister, as the case may be. It is understandable that when there is a rivalry of this nature between two children the first child has no hope of surpassing the second by being better than the second, and so he strives to excel him in the opposite direction, that is to say, by being as naughty as possible. It has been our experience that such naughty children can be turned into even better children than their brothers and sisters. It is also our experience that a strong desire for superiority may express itself in one extreme direction or the other. We see the same thing in school.

It is impossible to predict that two children will be exactly the same because they grow up under the same conditions. No two children grow up under exactly the same conditions. The character of a well-behaved child is greatly influenced by the presence of an ill-behaved one. As a matter of fact, there are many children who were originally well-behaved and who afterwards turned into problem children.

There is the case of a seventeen-year old girl who was a model child up to the time she was ten years old. She had a brother eleven years older who had been badly spoiled because he had been the only child for eleven years. The boy was not jealous of his sister when she arrived; he merely continued his usual behavior. When the little girl reached her tenth year the brother began to be away from home for long periods. She assumed the position of an only child, and this situation had the effect of making her want to have her own way at any price. She grew up in a rich home, so that when she was a child it was easy to fulfill her every desire. When she grew older this was not always possible and she began to show her dissatisfaction. She commenced to incur debts at an early age on the strength of her family's financial reputation, and in a short time she owed a considerable sum of money. This means nothing more than that she chose another road to fulfill her wishes. Her good behavior vanished when her mother refused to accede to her demands. There were quarrels, tears and the girl developed into a most unpleasant character.

The general conclusion to be drawn from this case and other cases resembling it, is that a child can satisfy his superiority striving by good behavior and that we are therefore never sure whether such good behavior will continue when there is a change in the situation. The advantage of our psychological questionnaire is that it gives us a more comprehensive picture of the child and his activities, as well as his relation to his environment and to all its members. There will always be certain indications of his style of life, and when we have studied the child and the information gained from the questionnaire we will find that his character traits, emotions and style of life are all tools used by him to promote his striving for superiority, increase his feeling of importance and obtain prestige in his world.

There is a type of child frequently met with in school who seems to contradict this description. This is the indolent child who is reserved, impervious to knowledge, discipline, or correction, who lives in a world of his own fantasy, and at no time displaying a striving for superiority. With enough experience, however, it is possible to perceive that this is also a form of striving, even though an absurd one. Such a child has no faith in his ability to achieve success by the usual means, and as a result he avoids all means and opportunities for improvement. He isolates himself and gives the impression of a hardened character. This hardness, however, does not include his whole personality; behind it one usually can find an extraordinarily sensitive, trembling spirit which needs this outer callousness to protect itself from hurt. He encloses himself in an armor and nothing can come near him.

When one succeeds in finding a way to induce this type to speak, one finds that he is very much occupied with himself, daydreams constantly and creates fantasies in which he always appears great or superior. Reality is far from the daydreams of such children. They make believe that they are heroes, conquering all others; or tyrants who have robbed all others of power; or martyrs helping the suffering. The inclination to play the savior is to be found frequently among children, not only in their daydreaming but in their actions. There are children who can be depended upon to spring to the rescue when another is in danger. Children who played the role of rescuer in their daydreams train themselves for the part in reality and, when not too discouraged, act the part when the opportunity offers.

Certain daydreams recur continually. In Austria during the time of the monarchy there were many children who had daydreams of saving the king or one of the princes from danger. The parents, of course, never know that their children have such ideas. All that is to be seen is that children who day-dream a lot cannot adjust themselves to reality and are unable to make themselves useful. In such cases there is a wide gap between fantasy and reality. Children sometimes choose the middle road: they retain their daydreaming while making a partial adjustment to reality. Others make no adjustment at all and withdraw more and more from the world into a private world of their own creation, while still others want to have nothing to do with prod-ucts of the imagination and occupy themselves only with reality—stories of travel, or of hunting, history, etc.

There is no doubt that a child should have some imagination as well as a willingness to accept reality, but we must not forget that children do not regard these things as simply as we do and are prone to divide the world sharply into two ex-tremes. A most important fact which should be borne in mind in understanding children is that they have a strong tendency to divide everything into opposites (above or below, all good or all bad, clever or stupid, superior or inferior, all or nothing). Adults also use this same antithetic scheme of apperception. It is well known that it is difficult to rid ourselves of this manner of thinking; for instance, to regard hot and cold as opposites when we know scientifically that the only difference is a difference in degree of temperature. Not only do we find this antithetic scheme of apperception very frequently among children but we also find it in the beginnings of philosophical science. The early days of Greek philosophy are dominated by this idea of opposites. Even to-day almost every amateur philosopher tries to measure values by means of opposites. Some of them have even established tables—life-death, above-below, and finally, man-woman. There is a significant similarity between the present childish and the old philosophic scheme of apperception, and we may assume that those people who are accustomed to divide the world into sharp contrasts have retained their childish way of thinking.

People who live according to such an antithetic device have a formula which can be expressed by the maxim "all or nothing." Of course it is impossible to realize such an ideal in this world, but nonetheless they regulate their lives according to it. It is impossible for human beings to have either all or nothing. There are a thousand and one gradations between these two extremes. This formula is to be found principally among those children who have a deep feeling of inferiority and who become inordinately ambitious as a compensation. There are several such characters to be found in history, for example, Cæsar, who was murdered by his friends when he sought for the crown. Many of the peculiarities and character traits of children can be traced to this idea of all or nothing—for example, stubbornness. There are so many proofs of this to be found in the lives of children that we have been led to conclude that such children have developed a private philosophy, or a private intelligence contrary to common sense. As an illustration we may cite the case of a four-year-old girl who was unusually stubborn and perverse. One day her mother brought her an orange and the child took it, threw it on the floor and said: "I don't want it when you bring it; I'll have it when I feel like having it!"

Indolent children who cannot have everything withdraw more and more into the emptiness of their daydreams, fantasies and castles-in-the-air. It must not be too quickly assumed, however, that such children are lost. We know very well that hypersensitive natures easily withdraw from reality since their personally created world of fantasy promises them a certain protection from further wounding. But this withdrawal does not necessarily bespeak complete maladjustment or unadaptability. A certain distance from reality is necessary not only for writers and artists but even for scientists, who also need a good imagination. The fantasies evoked in daydreams are nothing more nor less than a detour which an individual attempts to take to avoid the unpleasantnesses and possible failures in life. We must not forget that just those people who had rich imaginations and who were later able to combine their fantasies with reality became the leaders of mankind. They became leaders not only because of a better schooling, keener observation, but also because of their courage and the consciousness with which they approached the difficulties of life and successfully fought them. The biographies of great men often reveal that while they did not have much use for reality and were bad students as children, they did develop a remarkable ability to observe what went on around them; so that as soon as conditions became more favorable their courage grew to the point where they once more approached reality and took up the fight. Naturally, there is no rule as to how to make great men out of children. However, it is well to remember that we must never approach children brusquely, we must always encourage them, always try to explain to them the significance of real life so that they do not create a chasm between their fantasies and the world.

CHAPTER NINE

THE NEW SITUATION AS A TEST OF PREPARATION

NOT only is psychic life a unity, in the sense that all expressions of personality at any one time hang together, but it is also a continuity. The unfolding of personality in time takes place without sudden jumps. Present and future conduct is always consistent with past character. This is not to say that the events in an individual's life are mechanically determined by the past and by heredity, but it does mean that the future and past hang together without a break. We cannot jump out of our skins overnight, although we never know what is in our skins—that is to say we never know our full capabilities, until the moment that we express them.

In this fact of continuity without mechanical determinism, lies not merely the possibility of education and improvement, but also the possibility of detecting the state of character development at any given time. When an individual passes into a new situation, his hidden character traits come out. If we could directly experiment with individuals, we could find out their state of development by putting them through new and unexpected situations. Their conduct in such situations must be consistent with their past character, and it reveals their character in a way that ordinary situations do not.

In the case of children we get perhaps the best insights into their character at those moments of transition, when they pass from home to school, or when their home conditions are suddenly changed. It is then that the limitations in the child's character come out as clearly as an image on a photographic plate when it is put in a developing solution.

We had occasion once to observe an adopted child. He was incorrigible, had temper tantrums, and one could never tell what he was going to do next. When we spoke with the child he did not answer intelligently. He talked about things that had no connection with our questions. After we had considered the whole situation we thought: This child has been in the home of his foster parents for some months and maintains a hostile attitude toward them. Consequently he doesn't like it there.

It was the only conclusion that one could draw from the situation. His foster parents shook their heads at first and said that the child was well treated, in fact better than he had ever been treated before in his life. But that is not decisive. We often hear parents say: "We have tried everything with the child, gentleness and severity, and nothing has helped." Kindness by itself is not enough. There are children who react favorably to kindness, but we must not imagine that we have changed them. They believe that they are for a time in a favorable position, but basically they have remained the same and the disappearance of the kindness would at once bring back the old condition.

What is necessary is an understanding of how this child feels and thinks—how he interprets his situation—and not what his parents think. We pointed out to the foster parents that this child did not feel happy with them. We could not tell them whether or not he was justified in his attitude, but something must have happened to arouse such hate in the child. We told them that if they did not feel capable of correcting the child's mistakes and winning his love, they would have to give him away to some one else, because he would always rebel against what he considered an imprisonment. Later we heard that the boy had become a veritable fury, and he was considered actually dangerous. The child might have been slightly improved by gentle treatment but that would not have been enough because he did not understand the whole scheme which became clear to us as we elicited further information. The real explanation of the case follows: He grew up with the children of his foster parents and believed that they did not care for him as much as they did for their own children. That is certainly no reason for such temper tantrums, but the child wanted to get out of the house and consequently every act which would further his desire seemed to him suitable. He acted intelligently in the light of the goal he had placed for himself and we can disregard any consideration of possible feeble-mindedness. It took the family some time to realize that they would have to give him away if they felt incapable of changing his behavior.

When one punishes such a child for his lapses, the punishment is for him a good reason for continuing his rebellion. It is a confirmation of his feeling that he is right in rebelling. We have a sound basis for our views, and from this point it can be seen that all the child's errors are to be understood only as the results of a fight against the environment, the results of his meeting a new situation for which he had not been prepared. Childish as these mistakes are they need not surprise us, since we see the same childish manifestations in adult life.

The interpretation of gestures and unostentatious forms of expression is an almost unexplored field. Probably no one is in so good a position as the teacher to arrange all these forms into a scheme and to examine their connection with each other and their origin. It must be remembered that one form of expression may on different occasions have different meanings; that two children can do the same thing without having it mean the same. Furthermore the forms of expression in problem children are varied even when they arise from the same psychological cause. It is simply that there is more than one road to a certain goal.

We cannot speak here of right or wrong from the point of view of common sense. When children make a mistake it is because they have a mistaken goal. Consequently what proceeds as the result of a striving to this mistaken goal is also mistaken. It is a peculiarity in the nature of mankind that the possibilities for making mistakes are innumerable but that it has only one truth at its disposal.

There are several forms of expression to which no attention is paid at school but which are of significance. For example, there is the position in sleep. An interesting case is that of a fifteen-year-old boy who suffered from the hallucination that the then Emperor Francis Joseph I had died and had appeared to him as a ghost, ordering him to organize an army and proceed against Russia. When we came to his room at night to see how he slept we saw a striking picture. He was lying in bed in the position of Napoleon. When we saw him the next day his posture was similar to the military pose expressed in his sleeping position. The connection between the hallucination and his waking attitude seemed rather clear. We inveigled him into a conversation in which we tried to convince him that the Emperor still lived. He did not want to believe it. He told us that he had always been teased about his small stature when he waited on the guests in the café. When we asked him if he knew some one who had the same posture in walking he thought a little and then said, "My teacher,

Mr. Meier." We seemed to be on the right track and were able to get over the difficulty by conjuring up the figure of Meier as another little Napoleon. What was still more important was this item: The boy told us that he would like to become a teacher. This teacher, Meier, was his favorite and he would like to imitate him in everything. In short, the whole life story of this boy was summed up in his posture.

A new situation is a test of a child's preparedness. If a child has been well prepared, he meets new situations with confidence. If he lacks preparedness, a new situation brings a tension which leads to a feeling of incapacity. The feeling of incapacity distorts judgment, and the reaction is untrue—that is to say, it does not correspond to the demands of the situation—because it is not based on social feeling. In other words, a child's failure in school must be attributed, not only to the inefficiency of the school system, but to the primary deficiency in the child.

We must examine the new situation, not because we believe it to be the cause of deterioration in a child, but because we know that it shows more clearly the primary inadequate preparedness. Every new situation may be regarded as a test of preparedness.

In this connection we may again take up for discussion some points in the questionnaire (see Appendix I).

1. Since when has there been cause for complaint? Our attention is at once called to a new situation. When a mother remarks that her child was all right till he went to school, she tells us more than she really understands. The school has been too much for the child. It is not enough when the mother answers, "For the last three years." We must know what changes took place three years ago in the child's environment or in his own physical condition.

The first sign of a child's waning faith in himself is frequently found in his inability to adapt himself to school life. The initial failure is sometimes not taken seriously enough and it may mean a catastrophe for the child. We must find out how often a child has been spanked for receiving bad school marks, and what effect these marks or the spankings have had on his striving for superiority. The child may become convinced that he is incapable of accomplishment, especially if his parents are in the habit of saying, "You'll never amount to anything," or "You'll end up on the gallows."

Some children are spurred on by failure; others break down. Children who lose confidence in themselves and faith in the future must be encouraged. They must be treated gently, patiently and tolerantly.

A brusque explanation of sex may shock a child into confusion. The brilliant success of a sister or brother may deter him from further effort.

2. Was it noticeable before? This means, was the child's lack of preparedness noticeable up to the time of change in his situation? We get all kinds of answers to this question. "The child was disorderly," which means that the mother used to do everything for him. "He was always timid," which means great attachment to the family. When a child is described as weakly, we may assume that he was born with weak organs, was spoiled or pampered because of his weakness, or he may have been neglected on account of ugliness. This question also refers to a possible feeble-mindedness. The child may have developed very slowly so that he was suspected of being mentally weak. Even though he later grew out of this condition, he would still retain the feeling of having been pampered or

restricted, and these feelings would make much more difficult any attempt to cope with a new situation. If we are told that the child is cowardly and careless, we may be sure that he thereby secures the attention of another.

The first task of a teacher is to win the child, and thereafter to nourish his courage. When a child is clumsy the teacher must find out whether he is left-handed. If the child is clumsy to an exaggerated degree the teacher should find out whether the child fully understands his sexual role. Boys who grow up in a feminine environment, who avoid the company of other boys, who are teased and mocked and often treated like girls—such boys accustom themselves to the part of girls, and later develop rather stormy internal conflicts. Ignorance of the organic sexual distinction between male and female leads children to believe that it is possible to change their sex. But they eventually discover that their bodily constitution is unchangeable and try to compensate by developing either mental masculine or feminine traits, according to the sex to which they wish to belong. They express these tendencies in dress and deportment.

Some girls develop a loathing for feminine occupations. The chief reason is the supposed valuelessness of such work, which expresses indeed a basic failure of our civilization. The tradition still exists that men have privileges which are denied to women. Our civilization is distinctly to man's advantage and approves of certain rights which men assume for themselves. The birth of a son usually arouses more joy than the arrival of a daughter. This cannot but be a harmful influence on both son and daughter. The thorn of inferiority stings the girl very soon, while the boy is burdened with expectations. Girls are restricted in their development. There are countries in which this compulsion is no longer so noticeable; for example, in America. But in social relations no balance has yet been achieved, even in this country.

We are concerned here with the whole mentality of mankind which is mirrored in the children. The acceptance of the role of woman involves some hardship which occasionally incites revolt. This revolt expresses itself frequently in unruliness, stubbornness, indolence, all of which have to do with a striving for superiority. When such symptoms appear, the teacher must find out whether the girl is dissatisfied with her sex.

This particular dissatisfaction may grow to include all other fields, so that life in general becomes a burden. Occasionally we meet with the expression of the desire to live on another planet where mankind is not bi-sexual. Such erroneous thought processes can lead to various absurdities, or to complete apathy, criminality and even suicide. Punishment and lack of affection only strengthen the feeling of inadequacy.

Such unfortunate conditions can be avoided when the child learns in an unobtrusive fashion the difference between man and woman and is taught that each is worth as much as the other. It usually happens that the father seems to have a sort of superiority. The father appears to be the possessor, makes the rules, directs, explains to his wife and decides. Brothers try to be superior to their sisters, and make them dissatisfied with their sex by scorn and criticism. The psychologist understands that such conduct on the part of brothers springs from their own feeling of weakness. It is quite different to be able to do something than only to *seem* to be able. The argument that women have up to now not been able to point to great accomplishments is quite worthless. Women have not heretofore been reared to do great things. Men have put in the hands of women stockings to mend, and have tried to convince women that that was their work. This has been partly done away with, but the way we prepare girls to-day does not indicate that we expect anything extraordinary of them.

To hinder preparation and then adversely criticize inferior accomplishment is short-sighted. It is not easy to improve the present situation because it happens that not only fathers but mothers as well look upon masculine privileges as justified and rear their children according to this idea. They teach their children that masculine authority is right and their boys demand obedience and the girls resign themselves to it. Children should know at as early an age as possible to which sex they belong, and also that their sex is unchangeable. Women, as we have said, have developed resentment against the masculine assumption of authority and superiority. Where this resentment is so great that it is expressed in a woman's refusing to accept her sex and striving to be as much like a man as possible, Individual Psychology has called it the "masculine protest." Secondary symptoms, such as deformity or incomplete development, often lead adults to doubt their sex in reference to anatomical completion (masculine physical characteristics in girls and feminine in boys). These beliefs are sometimes deeply imbedded and related to constitutional weaknesses. A childish bodily construction, more noticeable in the case of a man than a woman, gives rise to the remark that the man has feminine characteristics. This is untrue, for such a man resembles much more a child. A man whose body does not develop completely feels himself painfully inferior because the general ideal of our civilization is that of man full-grown, whose achievements must surpass those of woman. An incomplete development or lack of beauty in the case of a girl also leads frequently to an aversion to the problems of life because we overvalue beauty.

Disposition, temperament and feelings are tertiary sexual indications. Sensitive boys are called feminine; poised, self-confident girls are described as masculine. Such traits are never innate, they are always acquired. These characteristics in early childhood are remembered later and adults refer to the fact that they were peculiar as children, that they were reserved or behaved like boys or girls, as the case may be. They developed according to the interpretation of their respective sexual roles. The further question, how far sexual development and experience has gone, means that a certain understanding is expected at a certain age. I should say that at least ninety per cent of the children, when parents or educators finally explain sexual matters to them, have already learned the facts long before. No hard and fast rules concerning sexual explanation can be made, because one cannot predict what a child will accept, or will credit in such an explanation, or in general what effect it will have on him. As soon as the child asks for an explanation, it should be given after considering carefully the condition of the child at the time. Premature explanation is inadvisable, even though it does not always have a harmful effect.

The question of an adopted child or a step-child is a difficult one. Children belonging to either of these classes take good treatment as a matter of course and blame all severity on their special family position. Sometimes a child who has lost his mother attaches himself closely to his father. After a while the father marries and the child feels that he has been shut out and refuses to make friends with the stepmother. It is interesting to note that a few children regard their real parents as step-parents, which implies, of course, harsh criticism and complaint. Step-parents have acquired a bad reputation on account of the many fairy tales in which they are the evil characters. Fairy tales, it may be said in passing, are not perfect reading material for children. It is impossible to forbid them completely, because children learn a great deal about human nature from them. But it would be worth while to have corrective comments written to accompany certain stories and to prevent children from reading those tales which have in them cruelty or distorted fantasy. Fairy tales of strong men performing cruel deeds have been used occasionally to harden the child readers, to dwarf soft feelings—another mistaken idea springing from our hero worship. Boys think it unmanly to show sympathy. It is incomprehensible why tender emotion is scorned, since it is indubitably valuable when it is not misused—although any emotion can of course be misused.

Illegitimate children, too, are in an extremely difficult situation. It goes without saying that it is not right that the woman and the child should bear the burden of illegitimacy while the man goes scot free. The one who pays the greatest price is, of course, the child. No matter how one wants to help such children it is impossible to prevent their suffering, for their common sense soon tells them that all is not in order. They are scorned by their companions or else the laws of the country make living conditions hard, and illegitimacy is legally branded on them. Because of their sensitiveness they quarrel easily and develop a hostile attitude to the world, for in every language there are ugly, insulting and painfully degrading words for such children. It is easily understandable why there are so many orphans and illegitimate children among problem children and criminals. It is impossible to attribute these asocial tendencies in illegitimate or orphaned children to innate or inherited dispositions.

CHAPTER TEN

THE CHILD AT SCHOOL

WHEN a child enters school he finds himself, as we have said, in a situation that is wholly new to him. Like all new situations entrance into school can be regarded as a test of previous preparation. If the child has been properly trained he will pass the test in a normal manner; if not, the defects in his preparation will become clearly apparent.

We do not often take records of a child's psychological preparedness at the time he enters nursery school and elementary school, but such records, if we had them, would shed great light on behavior in adult life. Such "new situation tests" would be infinitely more revealing than ordinary tests of scholastic performance.

What is demanded of a child when he enters school? School work is a task that demands cooperation with the teacher and with the schoolmates, as well as an interest in the school subjects.

By the child's responses to this new situation we can gauge his degree of co-operative ability and his sphere of interest. We can tell in what subjects the child is interested; we can see whether he is interested in what another person says; we can tell whether he is interested in anything at all. We can ascertain all these facts by studying the attitude of the child, his posture and look, the way he listens, whether he approaches the teacher in a friendly manner, or whether he stays far away from him, etc.

How these details affect one's psychological development may be illustrated by the case of a certain man, who consulted a psychologist because he had difficulties in his profession. Looking back into his childhood, the psychologist discovered that he had grown up in a family in which all the other children were girls; also the parents died soon after he was born. When the time came to enter school, he did not know whether he should register in the girls' or in the boys' school. He was persuaded by his sisters to enter the girls' school, only to be dismissed from there in a very short time. We can imagine the impression it left on the child's mind.

Concentration on school subjects is largely dependent upon the child's interest in his teacher. It is part of the teacher's art to keep a child attentive, and to find out when a child is not attentive or is unable to concentrate. There are many children who come to school without any ability for concentration. They are generally the pampered children, who are dazed by the presence of so many strange persons. If the teacher should happen to be a little strict, it will appear as if such children have no memory. But this lack of memory is not so simple a fact as it is generally regarded. A child who is reproached by the teacher with having no memory has a memory for other things. He is even able to concentrate, but only for the situation in which he has been pampered at home. He is attentive to his desire to be pampered, but not for school work.

If such a child does not get on in school, if he has bad reports and does not pass his examinations, it is useless to criticize him or reproach him. Criticism and reproaches will not change his style of life. On the contrary such things will convince him that he is not fit for school and will make him develop a pessimistic attitude.

It is significant that pampered children, when they are won over by the teacher, are often very good pupils. They can work when they have a great advantage for themselves; unfortunately we cannot guarantee that they will always be pampered at school. If the child changes schools or changes teachers, or even if he does not make progress in a particular subject (and arithmetic is always a dangerous subject for pampered children), he will suddenly come to a stop. He will not be able to go ahead because he has been accustomed to having everything made easy for him. He has never been trained to struggle and does not know how to struggle. He has no patience for meeting difficulties and forging ahead by conscious efforts.

We see, then, what is meant by sound preparation for school. In bad preparation, we can always see the influence of the mother. We can understand how she was the first to awaken the interest of the child, and thus had the crucial responsibility of directing that interest into healthy channels. If she failed in her responsibility, as she often did, the result was made evident in the child's behavior at school. Besides the mother's influence there is the whole complex of family influences—the influence of the father, the rivalry of the children, which we have analyzed in other chapters. Then, too, there are the outside influences, the bad circumstances and prejudices, about which we shall speak more at length in a succeeding chapter.

In short, with all these circumstances that account for the bad preparation of the child, it is foolish to judge the child on the basis of his scholastic record. Rather should we take the school reports as so many indications of the child's present psychological condition. It is not the marks that he gets but what they indicate as to his intelligence, interest, ability at concentration, etc. Scholastic tests should not be interpreted differently from such scientific tests as intelligence tests, despite the difference in their construction. In both cases the emphasis should be on what is revealed as to the child's mind, and not as to the quantity of facts that are written down.

In recent years the so-called intelligence tests have been very much developed. They have a great weight with teachers, and sometimes they are worth while, since they reveal things not shown by the ordinary tests. Once in a while they prove the salvation of the child. Thus when a boy has had bad school reports and the teacher has wanted to put him into a lower class, the intelligence may suddenly reveal a higher rating. The child, instead of being put back, is allowed to skip a grade. He feels successful, and thereafter acts differently.

We do not wish to undervalue the function of an intelligence test and of an I.Q., but we must say that when a test is used neither the child nor the parents should know the I.Q. Neither the parents nor the child know the true value of an intelligence test. They imagine that it represents a final and complete point of view, that it indicates the fate of the child, who is henceforth limited by it. In reality the findings revealed by intelligence tests are quite open to criticism if they are taken as absolute findings. A good rating on an intelligence test is no guarantee for later life, and on the other hand grown-up persons who are otherwise successful make low scores.

It has been the experience of Individual Psychologists that whenever intelligence tests reveal a great lack of intelligence, the scores can be improved if we find the right methods. One of these methods is to let the child play with the particular intelligence test until he finds out the right trick, as well as the right preparation for taking such an examination. In this way the child makes progress and increases his experience. He will make better scores on subsequent tests.

THE EDUCATION OF CHILDREN

It is a great question as to how children are influenced by the school routine, and whether they are not oppressed by the heavy school curriculum. We do not undervalue the subjects in the school curriculum, and we do not believe that the number of subjects taught should be decreased. It is of course important to teach subjects in a coherent manner so that the children see the purpose and practical value of their subject and do not regard it as purely abstract and theoretical. There is great discussion at the present time over the question, shall we teach the child to learn subjects and facts, or shall we educate the child's personality. We in Individual Psychology believe that the two can be combined.

As we have said, subjects of instruction should be made interesting and practical. Mathematics—arithmetic and geometry—should be taught in connection with the style and structure of a building, the number of people that can live there, etc. Some subjects can be taught together. In some of the more progressive schools we have experts who know how to teach subjects in interrelation. They take a walk with the children and find out that they are more interested in certain subjects than in others. They learn to combine instruction; they

THE EDUCATION OF CHILDREN

learn to combine, for example, instruction about the plant with the history of the plant, the climate of the country, etc. In this way they not only stimulate interest in subjects which would otherwise be uninteresting to the child, but they give him a coordinated and synthetic approach to things, which is the final aim of all education.

There is a point that educators must not overlook, and this is that children at school feel themselves to be in a personal competition. We can readily understand why this point is important. The ideal school class should be a unit, in which each of the children feels himself a part of the whole. The teacher should see to it that the rivalries and personal ambitions are kept within bounds. Children do not like to see others forge ahead, and either do not spare themselves to overtake their competitors or else suffer a relapse into disappointment and a subjective view of things. That is why the advice and direction of the teacher is so important—a proper word from him will transfer the energies of the child from competitive to cooperative channels.

In this connection the institution of modified schemes of self-government in classes is helpful. We do not have to wait until children are completely ready for self-government to institute schemes of this kind. We can allow the children at first to watch what is going on, or to act in an advisory capacity. If children are given complete self-government without preparation, we shall find that they are more severe and strict in their punishments than are the teachers, or even that they use their political functions for personal advantage and superiority.

As regards the progress of the children through school, we have to take into account both the point of view of the teacher and the point of view of the children. It is an interesting fact that children have very good judgment in this regard. They know who is the best in spelling, in drawing, in athletics. They can rate each other quite well. Sometimes they are not quite just to others, but they realize this, and try to be fair. The great difficulty is that they minimize themselves: they believe, "Now, I can never catch up." This is not true—they can catch up. The mistake in their judgment must be pointed out to them, otherwise it will become an *idée fixe* throughout life. A child who has such an idea will never progress but will always stay where he is.

The great majority of school children are nearly

always at the same level: they are the best or the worst or the average, and they stay that way. This state of things does not reflect so much the development of the brain, as it does the inertia of psychological attitudes. It is a sign that children have limited themselves and cease to be optimistic after the first few checks. But that fact that changes in relative position do take place once in a while is important: it shows that there is no fatality that governs the intellectual status of a child. Children should know of this, and be brought to understand its application in their own case.

Both the teacher and the children should also get rid of the superstition that the results accomplished by children with normal intelligence should be attributed to special heredity. This is perhaps the greatest mistake that is ever made in regard to the education of children—this belief in the inheritance of abilities. When Individual Psychology first pointed this out, people thought that it was simply an optimistic conjecture on our part, not a generalization based on science. But now more and more psychologists and psychiatrists are coming to accept this point of view. Heredity is too easy a scapegoat for parents, teachers and children. Whenever there are difficulties that require effort, they can always call upon heredity to relieve them of any responsibility for doing things. But we have no right to escape our responsibilities, and we should always be suspicious of any points of view that have the effect of releasing us from responsibilities.

No educator who believes in the *educative* value of his work, who believes in education as the training of character, can consistently accept the doctrine of heredity. We are not concerned with physical heredity. We know that organic defects, even differences in organic ability are inherited. But where is the bridge between the functioning of organs and the ability of the mind? In Individual Psychology we have insisted that the mind experiences the degree of ability possessed by the organs and has to reckon with it. Sometimes the mind reckons too much with it—in that it gets frightened by some organic disability, and the fright lasts long after the organic cause is removed.

People always like to trace things back to their origins and to seek the germs from which the phenomena developed. But this point of view, which we constantly use in evaluating the achievements of persons, is very misleading. The usual error in this mode of procedure is to neglect most of the ancestors, forgetting that if we are to construct family trees there are two parents at every generation. If we trace back five generations there are 64 ancestors, and among 64 ancestors one can doubtless find a clever person to whom to attribute the ability of his descendant. If we go back ten generations, we have 4,096 ancestors, and then there is no question but that we will find one very able person in the lot, if not more than one. It also must not be forgotten that the tradition given to a family by one very able person has an effect that resembles the working of heredity. We can thus understand how some families produce more able persons than other families. It is not inheritance, it is a very obvious and simple fact. Just consider how things used to work out in Europe when each child was forced to continue in the profession of the father. If we forget the social institutions the statistics of heredity can be made to look very formidable.

Next to the idea of heredity the problem that causes the greatest difficulties for the child is the punishment for bad school reports. If a child has bad school reports, he will also find himself not very well liked by the teacher. He thus suffers in school, and then comes home and finds new scenes and new reproaches from his parents. He is scolded by his mother and father, and very often he is spanked in addition.

School-teachers should keep in mind the aftermath of bad report cards. Some teachers believe that the child will struggle harder if he has to show a bad report at home. But they forget the particular home circumstances. In some homes the child is brought up in a rather cruel manner, and a child of such a home will think twice before bringing back a bad report. As a result he may not come at all, or sometimes he may be driven to the extremes of despair and commit suicide from fear of his parents.

Teachers are not responsible for the school system, but it is well that wherever possible they temper the impersonal severities of the system with a personal touch of sympathy and understanding. Thus a teacher could be milder with a particular pupil on account of his home environment, and by being milder could encourage him instead of driving him to despair. There is a heavy weight on the mind of a child who always gets bad reports and who continually is told by others that he is the worst pupil of the school until he believes it himself. If we identify ourselves with such a child we

178

can readily understand why he does not like school. It is only human. If any one were in a place where he was always criticized, had bad school reports, and lost the hope of ever catching up, he would not like the place and would try to escape from it. And so we should not be upset when we see such children staying away from school.

But while we should not be alarmed at such an occurrence we should realize its significance. We should realize that it means a bad beginning, especially if it happens in the period of adolescence. Such children are clever enough to protect themselves by forging report cards, playing truant, etc. In this way they meet others of their own kind, form gangs, and start out on the road that leads eventually to crime.

All this can be avoided if we accept the point of view of Individual Psychology that no child should be thought hopeless. We must feel that a method can always be found to help a child. Even in the worst of circumstances there is always a particular way of approach—but this of course needs to be found.

Of the bad results which follow from making children repeat classes, it is almost needless to speak. A teacher will agree that a child who repeats a class is a problem both for the school and for the family. This may not happen in every case, but the exceptions to the rule are very few. Most of those that repeat a class are chronic repeaters—they are always backward and present a problem which has always been evaded and never solved.

It is a difficult question when to let children repeat a class. There are teachers who manage to avoid the problem successfully. They use the vacation periods to train the child, to search out the mistakes in his style of life and correct them, and so they are able to let him go on into the next class. This method could be practiced more widely if we had the institution of special tutors at school. We have social workers and visiting teachers, but no tutors.

The institution of visiting teachers does not exist in Germany, and it would seem to us as if such teachers are not altogether necessary. The class teacher in the public school has the best view in regard to the child. He can know more than others what is going on if he looks rightly. There are some that say that the class teacher cannot know the individual pupils because the class is overcrowded. But if one observes how a child enters a school, one can see his style of life very soon and avoid many difficulties. This can be done even with a great crowd. One can educate a great number of children better if one understands them than if one does not understand them. Overcrowded classes are far from a blessing and should be avoided, but they are not an insuperable obstacle.

From the psychological point of view it is better that teachers do not change each year—or every six months as they do in some schools—but advance with the class. If a teacher could be with the same children for two, three or four years, it would be a great advantage all around. Then the teacher would have an opportunity for knowing all the children intimately. He would be able to know the mistakes in each one's style of life and correct them.

Children often skip classes. Whether there is any advantage in this is debatable. Often they fail to satisfy the high expectations that have been awakened in them by the skipping process. Skipping a class should be considered in the case of a child who is too old for his grade. It should also be considered in the case of a child who was backward before and has since developed and improved. Skipping a class should not be held out as reward for better marks or because the child knows more than others.

It is more to the advantage of a bright child if he devoted time to extra-school studies, like painting, music, etc. What the bright child learns in this way, is of advantage to the whole class, since it stimulates the others. It is not good to deprive a class of the better pupils. There are those who say that we always ought to promote the outstanding and bright children. We do not believe it. We believe rather that it is the bright children that push the whole class forward and give it a greater impetus for development.

It is interesting to examine the two types of classes we find at school—the advanced and the backward classes. One is amazed to find in the advanced classes a few children who are really feeble-minded, while the backward classes are peopled not with feeble-minded, as most persons think, but with children of poor families. Children of poor families get the reputation of being backward. The reason is that their preparation is not so good. And we can readily understand this. The parents have too much to do and are not able to devote any time to the children, or perhaps are not well enough educated for this purpose. Such children who lack psychological preparation should not be put into the backward classes. Being in a backward class is a stigma for a child, and the child is always ridiculed by his comrades.

A better way to take care of such children would be to apply the method of tutors, which we have already mentioned. Besides tutors, there should be clubs, where children could go and get extra tutoring. There they could do their home work, play games, read books, etc. In this way they would get a training in courage instead of a training in discouragement which is what they derive from classes for backward children. Such clubs, when combined with a greater abundance of playgrounds than we now have, would keep the children completely off the streets and away from bad influences.

The question of co-education comes up in all discussions of educational practice. As regards co-education, one may say that in principle we should promote it. It is a good way for girls and boys to get to know each other better. But, when one says co-education, and expects it to take care of itself, it is a great mistake. Co-education involves special problems that must be considered, or else the disadvantages will overbalance the advantages. There is one fact, for example, that people generally overlook, and this is that girls up to their sixteenth year develop more quickly than boys. If the boys do not realize this and see the girls get ahead faster than they do, they lose their balance and enter into a senseless race with the girls. Facts like these must be taken into consideration either by the administration or by the teacher in the class.

Co-education can be successfully achieved by a teacher who likes co-education and understands the problems involved. But a teacher who does not like co-education will feel burdened by the system, and in his class co-education will fail.

If the co-educational system is not properly administered and if the children are not rightly led and supervised, there will, of course, arise sex problems. We shall discuss sex problems more at length in a succeeding chapter. Here it may be pointed out that sex education in school presents a complicated problem. In fact the school is not the right place for imparting instruction about sex problems, because the teacher cannot know how the children will take his words when he speaks before a whole class. It is different if the children ask for information privately from the teacher. If a girl asks the teacher for facts, the teacher should answer rightly.

Returning now, after our digression on the more or less administrative phases of education, to the main heart of the problem, we may say that we can always find out how to educate children by consulting their interests and finding out the subjects in which they can be successful. Nothing succeeds like success. This is true of education as of other phases of human life. And it means that if a child is interested in one subject and is successful in it he will be stimulated to go on to other things. It is up to the teacher to utilize the pupils' successes as stepping-stones to greater knowledge. The pupil alone does not know how to do this—to lift himself by his bootstraps, so to speak, as all of us must do in ascending from ignorance to knowledge. But the teacher can do this, and if he does it he will find that the pupil will see the point and will cooperate.

What we have said about subjects of interest applies also to the sense organs of children. We must find out which sense organ is the most used and what type of sensations fascinate the child most. There are many children who are better trained in seeing and looking, others in listening, still others in moving, etc. In recent years the so-called manual schools have come into favor, and they utilize the sound principle of combining subjects of instruction with the training of the eyes, ears and hands.

The success of these schools is an indication of the importance of harnessing the physical interests of the child.

If a teacher finds a child of the visual type, he should understand that he will have things easier in subjects in which he has to use his eyes—as for example geography. It will be better for him to see than to listen to a lecture. This is a sample of the sort of insight into the problems of a particular child that a teacher should have. There are many other such insights which the teacher can get in his first look at the child.

In short the ideal teacher has a sacred and fascinating task. He moulds the minds of children, and the future of mankind is in his hands.

But how shall we pass from the ideal to the actual? It is not enough to envisage educational ideals. We must find a method to advance their realization. Long ago, in Vienna, the present writer started out to find such a method, and the result was the establishment of advisory clinics or guidance clinics in the schools.*

---

* See "Guiding the Child," by Alfred Adler and Associates, Greenberg: Publisher, *New York*, which gives a detailed account of the history, technique and results of these clinics.

THE EDUCATION OF CHILDREN

The purpose of these clinics is to put the knowledge of modern psychology at the service of the educational system. A competent psychologist who understands not only psychology, but the life of the teachers and parents as well, joins with the teachers and holds a consultation clinic on a certain day. On that day the teachers will have a meeting, and each one will bring up his particular cases of problem children. They will be cases of lazy children, children who corrupt the class, children who steal, etc. The teacher describes his particular cases, and then the psychologist will contribute his own experiences. Then the discussion starts. What are the causes? When did the situation develop? What should be done? The family life of the child and his whole psychological development is analyzed. With their combined knowledge, the group comes to a decision as to what should be done with a particular child.

At the next session the child and the mother are both present. The mother will be called in first, after the manner of influencing her has been settled. The mother listens to the explanation of why the child has failed. Then the mother tells her side of the story, and a discussion starts between the mother and the psychologist. Generally the mother is quite happy to see all these signs of interest in her child's case, and is glad to co-operate. If the mother is unfriendly and antagonistic, then the teacher or the psychologist begins to speak about similar cases and other mothers until the resistance is overcome.

When, finally, the method of influencing the child is agreed upon, the child enters the room. He sees the teacher and the psychologist, and the psychologist talks to him but not about his mistakes. The psychologist speaks as in a lecture, analyzing objectively—but in a manner that the child can grasp—the problems and the reasons and the ideas that are responsible for the failure to develop properly. The child is shown why he felt himself curtailed and other children preferred, how he came to despair of success, etc.

This method has been followed for nearly fifteen years, and the teachers that have been trained in this work are quite happy and would not think of dropping the work that they have been carrying on for four, six and eight years.

As for the children, they have gained doubly from this work: Those that were originally problem children have been made whole—they have learned the spirit of co-operation and courage. The others, too, who have not been called into the consultation clinics, have also benefited. When a situation arises in the class that threatens to become a problem, the teacher will propose that the children talk the matter out. The teacher, of course, directs the discussion, but the children participate and have full opportunity for expression. They begin to analyze the causes of a problem—say, laziness in the class. In the end they will reach some conclusion, and the lazy child, who does not know that he is meant will, nevertheless, learn a great deal from the discussion.

This summary account will give an indication of the possibilities that can be realized from the fusion of psychology and education. Psychology and education are two phases of the same reality and the same problem. To direct the mind we need to know its workings, and he who knows the mind and its workings cannot help but use his knowledge for directing the mind to higher and more universal goals.

CHAPTER ELEVEN

INFLUENCES FROM OUTSIDE

THE psychological and educational outlook of Individual Psychology is broad enough not to neglect the consideration of "influences from outside." The old type of introspective psychology was so narrow that, in order to take care of the fact it had left out, Wundt found it necessary to invent a new science, Social Psychology. This is not necessary with Individual Psychology, which is at one and the same time individual and social. It does not concentrate upon the individual mind to the exclusion of the environment which stimulates the mind, nor upon the environment to the exclusion of its significance to particular minds.

No educator or teacher should believe that he is the only educator of a child. The waves of outside influence stream into the psyches of the children and mould the children directly or indirectly —that is to say, by influencing the parents and bringing them to a certain state of mind which is transferred to the children. All this cannot be avoided, and it must therefore be taken into account.

First of all the educator must take into account economic circumstances. We must remember, for example, that there are families living for generation upon generation under very pressing circumstances—families that carry on their struggle with a sense of bitterness and sorrow. They are so much affected by this sorrow and bitterness that they cannot educate the child to take a healthy and co-operative attitude. They are living on the limits of the human mind, where human beings cannot work along co-operative lines because they are always panic-stricken.

And then, too, we must not forget that a long period of semi-starvation or bad economic circumstances influences the physical life of both parents and children, and this in turn has an important psychological impact. We see this in the children born in postwar Europe. They are much more difficult to bring up than previous generations. Besides economic circumstances and their effect on child development, we must not forget the effect of parental ignorance of physical hygiene. This ignorance goes hand in hand with the timid and coddling attitude of parents. Parents want to pamper the children and are afraid to cause them any pain. Sometimes they are careless, and they imagine, for example, that a curvature of the spine would be outgrown. They do not call for the doctor at the right time. This is, of course, a mistake, especially in cities where medical service is always available. A bad physical condition if not corrected in time may lead to a severe and dangerous illness, which may leave bad psychological scars. All illness is always a "dangerous corner" psychologically, and is to be avoided as much as possible.

If these dangerous corners cannot be avoided they can be made much less dangerous by developing in children the attitude of courage and social-mindedness. In fact it may be said that a child is psychologically affected by illness only in so far as he is not social-minded. A child that is brought up in an environment in which he feels himself a part of the whole will not be affected by a dangerous illness as would a pampered child.

Case histories often show the beginning of psychological troubles after such diseases as whooping cough, encephalitis, chorea, etc. One imagines that it is these illnesses which are the causes of psychological difficulties. But they are really only the occasions that bring out the hidden character flaws in the child. During his illness the child feels his power, and discovers how he can rule the family. He has seen terror and anxiety on the parents' faces during the illness, and knows that it is all on his account. After the illness he wants to continue to be the center of attention, and does this by trying to dominate the parents with his whims and demands. This, of course, happens with a child who has never been socially trained and needs only the occasion to manifest his egoistic strivings.

On the other hand it is interesting to note that sometimes an illness may be the occasion of an improvement in the character of the child. There is the case of a second child of a school-teacher. The teacher had been very much concerned over this boy, and had not known what to do with him. He would run away from home at times, and was always the worst pupil in his class at school. One day, just as the father was about to send him away to a reformatory, the boy was discovered to be suffering from tuberculosis of the hip. This is a disease which requires the constant care of the parents over a long period. When the boy finally recovered, he became the best child in the family. All that the boy needed was the extra attention from the parents that was provided by the illness. The reason he had been disobedient before was because he had always felt himself to be in the shadow of a brilliant older brother. Since he could not be appreciated like his brother, he was always fighting. But the illness convinced him that he, too, could be appreciated by his parents in the way that his older brother was, and so he learned to behave well.

As regards illness there is also to be noted that children's minds are often deeply impressed with the memory of the illnesses they have gone through. Children are surprised and astonished that there can be such things as dangerous illness and death. The mark that is left on their minds comes out later on in life, for we find many persons who are interested only in sickness and death. Part of these persons have found the right way to harness their interest in sickness—they may be doctors or nurses. But many others are always trembling, and sickness becomes an obsession with them which stands in the way of their useful work. An examination of the biographies of more than a hundred girls revealed that nearly fifty per cent confess that the greatest fear they have in life is the thought of illness and death.

Parents should see to it that children are not too

much impressed by their childhood sicknesses. They should prepare their minds for such facts and spare them sudden shocks. They should give them the impression that life is limited but yet long enough to be worth while.

Another "dangerous corner" of childhood life is the meeting with strangers, acquaintances or friends of the family. The mistakes that are made in the encounters with such persons are due to the fact that such persons are not really interested in the children. They like to amuse the children or do things which can influence them very much in a short time. They praise the children very highly, and thus get them to be conceited. In the short time they are with them they manage to pamper them and thus to make trouble for their regular educators. All this should be avoided. No stranger should interfere in the educational methods of the parents.

Again, strangers very often misunderstand the sex of a child and call the boy "a pretty girl" or vice versa. This, too, should be avoided, for the reasons which we discuss in the chapter on adolescence.

The general environment of the family is naturally important because it gives the children an indication of the extent to which the family takes part in social life. It gives them, in other words, the first impressions about co-operation. Children who grow up in an isolated family draw a sharp line between members of the family and outside persons. They feel as if there is a chasm separating the home and the outside world, which of course they regard in a hostile light. An isolated family life does not promote social relations and it inclines the children to be always suspicious and to look out only for their own interests. In this way it handicaps the development of social-mindedness.

A child at the age of three should be already prepared to join with other children in games and should not be scared by the presence of strangers. Otherwise the child will later turn out to be bashful and self-conscious, and will take a hostile attitude to others. Generally this trait is to be found among pampered children. Such children always want to "exclude" others.

If a parent occupies himself early with the correction of such traits he can be sure that the child will be spared a great deal of trouble later on. If a child has had a good up-bringing in his first three or four years—if he has been trained to play with others and to join in the common spirit—he will be spared not only bashfulness and egotism, but also a possible neurosis and even insanity. Insanity and neuroses occur only in the case of persons who live in an isolated manner, who are not interested in others, and who have not the right knack for co-operation.

While we are on the subject of family environment, we may mention the difficulties which arise as a result of a change of economic circumstances. If a family had once been rich, particularly when the child was very young, and then lost its money, there is obviously a difficult situation. Such a situation is hardest on a pampered child, for he is not prepared for circumstances under which he cannot get as much attention as before. He misses his past advantages and repines over them.

If a family suddenly becomes rich, there are again difficulties in the bringing up of the children. Here the parents are not prepared for the proper use of their wealth, and they especially make mistakes in regard to the children. They want to give the children a good time, they want to pamper them and spoil them because they feel they now need not stint on anything. As a result we find problem children very often among families that are newly rich. The son of a newly rich father is a notorious instance of this type of problem child.

Such difficulties and even disasters can be avoided if the child is properly trained in co-operation. All these situations are like open doors through which a child escapes the necessary training in co-operation, and we must be specially on the watch on that account.

Not only are children influenced by abnormalities in material circumstances, as poverty and sudden riches, but they are also influenced by abnormalities in psychological circumstances. We have in mind psychological prejudices which arise out of the family situation. These prejudices may arise out of personal acts, as, for example, if the father or mother has done something that is socially disgraceful. In that case the child's mind will be greatly affected. The child will face the future in fear and trepidation. He will want to hide himself from his fellows and will be afraid of being discovered to be the child of such a parent.

The parents have a responsibility not only to provide an education in reading, writing and arithmetic for their child, but also to give him the proper psychological basis of development so that he will not have to bear greater difficulties than others. Thus, if a father is a drunkard, or if he is high-tempered, he must remember that it all affects the child. If the marriage is an unhappy one, if the husband and wife constantly quarrel, it is the child who again pays.

These childhood experiences are like living inscriptions in the soul of the child, and he cannot forget them very easily. He can, of course, obviate their effects if he has been trained in co-operation. But the very situations which create these trials for the child prevent him from getting that training from the parents. That is why there has been in recent years a concerted movement to organize child guidance clinics in the schools. If the parent, for one reason or another, falls down on his task, his work must be taken over by a psychologically-trained teacher, who can guide the child to a healthy life.

Besides the prejudices which arise from personal circumstances there are the prejudices due to nationality, race and religion. One will always find that such prejudices affect not merely the child who is humiliated, but also the others, the aggressive ones who do the humiliating. They become arrogant and conceited; they believe that they belong to a privileged group, and when they try to live up to the privilege which they have erected for themselves, they end up as failures.

The prejudices between nations and races are of course the basic causes of war—that great scourge of mankind which must be abolished if progress and culture are to be saved. The task for the teacher is to show war in its true light, and not to give the child an easy and cheap opportunity of expressing his superiority striving by playing with guns and swords. This is not the proper preparation for a cultured life. There are many boys who join the army as a result of the military education of childhood; but besides those that join the army there are a hundred times as many who are psychologically crippled for the rest of their life by their childhood warrior games. They always go through life like warriors—with chips on their shoulders— and they never learn the art of getting along with their fellow men.

Around Christmas time and other seasons for toys, parents should especially keep an eye on the type of toys and games that are put into the children's hands. They should get rid of weapons and war games, as well as of all the books that worship war heroes and deeds of fighting.

THE EDUCATION OF CHILDREN

As regards the selection of proper toys, a great deal could be said, but the principle is that we should select the type of toys that will stimulate the child to be co-operative and constructive in his occupations. One can well understand that games in which a child can work and build up things are more worth while than ready-made or finished toys, which require the child merely to fondle a doll or an imitation dog, etc. Incidentally, as regards animals, children should be instructed to regard an animal not as toy or a game, but as a comrade of human beings. He should not be afraid of animals nor should he boss them or be cruel to them. Whenever children exhibit cruelty to animals one may suspect in them a desire to dominate and bully persons weaker than themselves. If there are animals, —birds, dogs, and cats—in the house, the children should be taught to regard them as living beings who feel and have pain in a way similar to human beings. Proper comradeship with animals may be regarded as a preparatory stage for social co-operation with human beings.

In the environment of children there are always relatives. First of all are the grandparents, and we have to consider their plight and situation in a dis-

interested manner. The position of grandparents
is something of a tragedy in our culture. When
people grow up, they should have room to expand,
they should have more occupations and interests.
But just the reverse happens in our society. Old
people feel put back, so to speak, relegated to a
corner. It is a pity because such persons could accomplish much more and could be infinitely happier if they had more of an opportunity for working and striving. One should never advise a man
at the age of 60, 70 or even 80 to retire from his
business. It is much easier to continue in business
than to change one's whole scheme of life. But owing to our mistaken social customs we put old people on the shelf while they are still full of activity.
We give them no opportunity for continued self-
expression. As a result, what happens? The mistakes that we visit on the grandparents rebound on
the children. The grandparents are always in the
position of having to prove—what they should not
have to prove—that they are still alive and count
in the world. In trying to prove this they are always interfering with the education of the grand-
children. They pamper the children terribly. It is
a disastrous way of attempting to prove that they
still know how to bring up children.

We should avoid hurting the feelings of these good and kind old people. But while they should be given an opportunity for more activity, they should be taught that children should grow up as independent human beings and should not be the playthings of other persons. They should not be exploited according to the exigencies of family politics. If the old people have arguments with the parents, let them win or lose the arguments but not try to put the children on their side.

How often do we find, when we study the biographies of psychological patients, that they were the favorites of their grandmothers or grandfathers! We immediately understand how this contributed to their childhood difficulties. Either their favoritism meant pampering or it meant stirring up rivalries and jealousies in reference to the other children. Also many children say to themselves, "I was the favorite of my grandfather," and feel hurt if they are not the favorite of other persons.

Among the other relatives who play a great role are the "brilliant cousins." They may be set down as a great nuisance. Sometimes they are not only brilliant but are also beautiful, and we can readily see what trouble it creates for a child to be reminded that he has a brilliant or beautiful cousin.

If he is courageous and social-minded he will understand that to be bright means simply to train better, and he will look for a way of overtaking the brilliant cousin. But if he believes, as most often happens, that brilliance is a blessing from nature—that people are born brilliant—then he will feel inferior and badly treated by fate. In this way his whole development will be retarded. As for beauty, which is to be sure a gift of nature but one that is constantly overvalued in our civilization, we can also see the mistakes in a child's style of life which are likely to arise when the child smarts under the painful thought that he or she has a beautiful cousin. Even after twenty years people still feel keenly the childhood envy of a beautiful cousin.

The only way to combat the ravages of this cult of beauty is to teach children that health and the ability to get along with one's fellow beings are more important than beauty. There is no gainsaying the fact that beauty is of value, and that it is more desirable to have a beautiful race of persons than an ugly race. But in any rational planning of things one value cannot be isolated from the rest and held up as the supreme goal. This is what happens with beauty. That beauty is not sufficient for a rational and good life is evidenced by the fact that we find among criminal types some very handsome boys, as well as others that are quite ugly. We can understand how these handsome boys may have become criminals. They knew they were handsome and they thought everything would come their way. They were, therefore, not prepared properly for life. Later on, however, they found they could not solve their problems without effort, and so they took the road of least resistance. As the poet Virgil said, *"facilis descensus Averno,"*—the descent to hell is easy. . . .

A word should be said about reading matter for children. What kinds of books should be given to children? What should be done with fairy tales? How should a book like the Bible be read to them? The main point here is that we generally overlook the fact that a child understands things in a wholly different way from an adult. We also overlook the fact that each child grasps things along the line of his own particular type of interest. If he is a timid child he will find in the Bible and in fairy tales stories that approve his timidity and make him always dread dangers. Fairy tales and Bible passages always need to be commented upon and interpreted so that the child gets the meaning that is intended and not the one that his subjective fancy dictates.

Fairy tales are of course enjoyable reading—even adults can read them with profit. But there is one point that needs to be corrected about them, and that is the sense of remoteness from particular times and places. Children seldom understand the differences of ages and the differences of cultures. They read a fairy tale which has been written in a totally different age and they do not make allowance for the difference in outlook. There is always the prince, and the prince is always praised and decorated, and his whole character is presented in a very alluring fashion. The circumstances described of course never existed, but they represent the fictional idealization proper to a certain period when it was necessary to worship the prince. Children should be told about such things. They should be told about the make-believe which is behind the magic; otherwise they may grow up always looking for an easy way out of things, like a certain boy of twelve, who, when asked what he wanted to be, said, "I want to be a magician."

Fairy tales, when properly commentated, can be used as a vehicle for instilling in children the sense of co-operation as well as for enlarging their outlook. As regards motion pictures, it may be said that there is no danger in taking a child of a year to see a film, but children of a later age will always misunderstand the pictures. Even fairy tale plays are often misunderstood by them. Thus a child at the age of four saw a certain fairy tale performed in a theatre. Years later he still believed that there were women in the world who sell poisoned apples. Many children do not understand the theme rightly, or else they make sweeping generalizations. It is up to the parent to explain things until he is sure they have understood rightly.

The reading of newspapers is one outside influence that can well be spared children. Newspapers are written for adults and do not have the child's point of view. There are in certain places special children's newspapers, and these are all to the good. But as for the ordinary newspaper, it gives a distorted picture of life to the unprepared child. The child gets to believe that our whole life is full of murders, crimes and accidents. Accident reports are specially depressing to young children. We can gather from remarks of grown up persons how much they were afraid of fire during childhood, and how this fear has continued to obsess their minds.

These examples comprise only a small selection of the outside influences which the parent and educator have to consider in the education of children. They are, however, the most important, and they illustrate the general principles involved. Again and again the Individual Psychologist has to insist upon the watchwords, "Social Interest" and "Courage." Here, as in other problems, the same slogans hold good.

CHAPTER TWELVE

ADOLESCENCE AND SEX EDUCATION

WHOLE libraries have been written about adolescence. The topic is indeed an important one, but not altogether in the way people imagine it. Adolescents are not all alike: we find all varieties of children in that class—striving children, clumsy children, children that are neatly dressed, children that go around very dirty, etc. We also find grown up persons and even old people who look and act like adolescents. From the point of view of Individual Psychology this is not very surprising, and it means simply that these grown up persons have stopped at a certain stage of development. In fact adolescence is, for Individual Psychology, simply a stage of development through which all individuals must pass. We do not believe that any stage of development, or any situation, can change a person. But it does act as a test—as a *new situation,* which brings out the character traits developed in the past.

Take, for example, a childhood in which the child has been closely watched and observed, a childhood in which the child has not enjoyed much power and has not been able to express what he wants. In the stage of adolescence, where there is a rapid biological and psychological development, such a child will act as if he has lost his chains. He will go ahead quickly and his personality will develop along sound lines. On the other hand there will be other children who will begin to stop and look back, and by looking back towards the past they will fail to find the right way in the present. They are not interested in life, and become very reserved. It is a sign, in their case, not of energies held in leash in a repressed childhood and finding their release in adolescence, but rather of a pampered childhood which has deprived them of the proper preparation for life.

In adolescence we are able to read a person's style of life better than ever before. The reason is, of course, that adolescence is nearer the front of life than is childhood. We can now see better how he will behave towards science. We can see whether he can make friends easily, whether he can be a fellowman who is socially interested in others.

Sometimes this social interest, so far from being absent, takes on an exaggerated expression, and we meet with adolescents who have lost the sense of balance and want only to sacrifice their lives for others. They are over-adjusted socially, and this, too, may prove an obstacle to their development. We know that if a person really wants to be interested in others and work for the common cause, he must first take care of himself. He must have something to give of himself, if the giving is to mean anything.

On the other side, we see many youths in the period between fourteen and twenty who feel altogether lost socially. At fourteen they have left school and have thus lost touch with all their old comrades; and it will take them a long time to form new ties. In the meantime they feel wholly isolated.

Then there is the question of occupation. Here again adolescence is revealing. It will reveal the attitude formed in the style of life. We will find some youths becoming very independent and working marvelously. They will show that they are on the proper road to development. Others, however, will come to a stop in this period. They will not find the right occupation for themselves; they will always be changing—either changing trades or changing schools, etc. Or else they will be idle and will not want to work at all.

None of these symptoms is created in adolescence, but they are merely brought more clearly to the surface in this period—they have been prepared before. And if a person really knows a particular child, he can predict how he will behave in the period of adolescence when he is given opportunities to express himself more independently than in the period when he was watched, guarded and restricted.

We turn to the third fundamental problem of life—love and marriage. What does the adolescent's answer to this problem reveal about his personality? Again there is no break with the pre-adolescent period, only a heightened psychological activity which makes the answers more clear-cut than before. We will find that some adolescents are wholly sure as to how they have to behave. They are either romantic on the problem of love or are very courageous. In any case they find the right norm of behavior towards the other sex.

There is another group at the other extreme, who become terribly shy on the question of sex. Now that they are much nearer the front, so to speak, they show up their lack of preparation. The indica-

THE EDUCATION OF CHILDREN

tions about personality that we derive from the
period of adolescence make possible a reliable judgment as to the course of behavior in later life. We
know what must be done if we want to change the
future.

If an adolescent shows himself very negativistic
in regard to the other sex, we will find, if we trace
back his life, that he was probably a fighting child.
Perhaps he was one that felt depressed because another child was preferred. As a result he believes
now that he must step forward very strongly, that
he must be arrogant and deny all the calls of sentiment. His attitude to sex is thus a reflex of his childhood experiences.

In the period of adolescence we often find the desire to leave home. This may be due to the fact that
the child has never been satisfied with home conditions, and is now aching for the first opportunity to
break home ties. He does not want to be supported
any more, although it is really for the best interests
of both the child and the parent that the support be
continued. Otherwise, in case things go wrong with
the child, the lack of help from the parents becomes
an alibi for his failure.

The same tendency, expressed in a smaller degree, is found in the case of children who remain at

home, but use every possible occasion to stay out at night. It is, of course, much more alluring to go out at night and seek amusement than to stay quietly at home. It is also an implicit accusation against the home, and a sign that at home the child does not feel free, but is always guarded and watched. Thus he has never had the occasion to express himself and to find out his own mistakes. The period of adolescence is a dangerous time to make a beginning in this direction.

Many children also feel a sudden loss of appreciation more keenly in the period of adolescence than they would have felt before. Perhaps they had been good pupils at school and highly appreciated by their teachers; then they were suddenly transferred to a new school, to a new social environment or to a new occupation. And then, too, we know that often the best pupils at school do not continue to be the best in the period of adolescence. They seem to undergo a change, but in reality there is no change, only that the old situation did not show up their character as truly as the new situation.

From all this, it follows that one of the best preventives for the troubles of adolescence is the cultivation of friendship. Children should be good friends and comrades with one another. And this goes for members of the family as well as for people outside the family. The family should be a unit in which every one trusts the others. The child should trust his parents and his teachers. Indeed, in the period of adolescence only that type of parent and teacher can continue in his capacity of guide to the child who has hitherto been a comrade and sympathetic fellow-man to his charge. Any other kind of parent or teacher is immediately shut out by the child during this period; the child will not repose any confidences in him and will regard him as a complete outsider or even as an enemy.

Among girls, one will find that it is just at this time that they will reveal their dislike of the feminine role, and that they will seek to imitate boys. It is of course much easier to imitate boys in the adolescent vices—that is, in smoking, drinking and joining gangs—than in the virtues of hard work. Also, the girls have the excuse that if they did not copy such practices the boys would not be interested in them.

If we analyze this masculine protest of the adolescent girl we shall find that the girl in question never liked the feminine role from early childhood. Hitherto, however, her dislike was covered up, and it comes out clearly only in adolescence. That is why it is so important to observe the behavior of girls at this time, for it is then that we can find out how they stand in regard to their sex role of the future.

Boys at this age often like to play the role of a man who is very wise, very brave and self-confident. Another class is afraid of their problems, and do not trust themselves to be really and completely men. If there has been any defect in their education for the male role this is the time it will come out. They will show themselves effeminate, they will like to behave like girls, and they will even imitate the vices of girls—being coquettish, liking to pose, etc.

Parallel with this feminine extreme among boys, we may also find boys who excel in the typically boyish traits, which may be carried to the extreme of vice. They will excel in drinking and in sexual excesses. Sometimes they will even begin to commit crimes merely out of a desire to show off their manliness. Such vices are found among boys who want to be superior, who want to be leaders and who want to astonish their comrades.

In this type, however, despite the bravado and ambition, there is often a secret trait of cowardice. We have had recently some notorious examples of this in America—types like Hickman, Leopold and Loeb. If we examine such careers we shall find that they were prepared for an easy life and were always looking for easy successes. Such types are active but not courageous—just the right combination for criminality.

We often find children at the adolescent age striking their parents for the first time. One who does not look for the hidden unity behind their actions will imagine that these children have suddenly changed. But, if we study what happened before, we realize that the individual is quite the same in character, only that he now has more power and more possibilities for action.

Another point to be considered is that in the period of adolescence every child feels that he is confronted with a test—he feels that he must prove that he is no longer a child. This is of course a very treacherous feeling, for every time we feel that we must prove something, we are likely to go too far. And so the child also goes too far.

This is indeed the most significant symptom of adolescence. And the way to counteract it is by explaining to the youth that he does not have to convince us that he is no longer a child; we do not need the proof. By telling him this we may avoid the exaggerated features we have mentioned.

Among girls we often find a type that is inclined

to exaggerate sex relations and become "boy-crazy." These girls are always fighting with their mothers and always believe themselves to be suppressed (and perhaps they are really suppressed); they will have relations with any man they meet in order to spite the mother. They are quite happy in the knowledge that the mother will be pained if she should find out. Many an adolescent girl has had first sex relations with a man after running out of the house on account of a quarrel with the mother, or because the father was too severe.

It is ironical to think of girls being suppressed by their parents in order that they may be good girls, and then turning out bad because of the parents' lack of psychological insight. The fault in such cases does not lie with the girls but with the parents, because they have not properly prepared the girls for the situations they must meet. They have sheltered the girls too much before adolescence, and as a result they have failed to develop in them the judgment and self-reliance necessary for meeting the pitfalls of adolescence.

Sometimes the difficulties appear not in adolescence but after adolescence, in marriage. The principle is, however, the same. It is simply that the girls were fortunate enough not to meet an unfavorable situation in adolescence. But sooner or later an unfavorable situation is bound to occur, and it is necessary to be prepared for it.

A single case history may be cited here to illustrate concretely the problem of the adolescent girl. The girl in this case was fifteen years old and came from a very poor family. Unfortunately she had an older brother who was always sick and had to be nursed by the mother. The girl noticed the difference in attention from her early childhood. What complicated matters was the fact that when she was born the father was also sick, and the mother had to take care of both him and the brother. The girl had a double example of what it means to be nursed and to get attention, and it became her passionate longing to be cared for and to be appreciated by people. She could not find this appreciation in the family circle, especially as a younger sister was soon born into the family and deprived her of the little modicum of attention that she still had. Now as fate would have it, when the younger sister was born the father got well, so that the baby got more attention than she herself had received during her infancy. Children notice these things.

The girl made up for her lack of attention at home by striving hard at school. She made herself the best pupil in her class, and because she was such a good pupil it was proposed that she continue her studies and go through high school. But as she entered high school a change took place. Her studies were not so good, and the reason was that her new teacher did not know her and did not appreciate her. She, on her side, was eager for appreciation, but now she lacked it both at home and at school. She had to get her appreciation somewhere. And so she went out to look for a man who would appreciate her. She lived with the man for a fortnight. Then the man got tired of her. We could have predicted what would happen; we could have predicted that she would realize that this is not the appreciation she wanted. In the meantime the family became worried and started a search for her. Suddenly they received a letter from her, saying, "I have taken poison. Do not worry— I am happy." Suicide was obviously her next thought, after being defeated in her quest for happiness and appreciation. Nonetheless she did not commit suicide; she used suicide as a scare with which to bring about forgiveness from her parents. She continued to run around the streets until her mother found her and brought her home.

If the girl knew, as we know, that her whole life was dominated by the striving to be appreciated, then all these things would not have happened. Also if the teacher at the high school had realized that the girl had always been good in her studies and that all she needed was a certain measure of appreciation, the tragedy would again not have taken place. At any point in the chain of circumstances a proper handling of the girl could have prevented her going to ruin.

This brings up the matter of sex education. The subject of sex education has been frightfully exaggerated in recent times. There are many persons who are, if we may say so, insane on the subject of sex education. They want sex education at any and all ages, and they play up the dangers of sexual ignorance. But if we look into our own past and into the past of others we do not see such great difficulties nor such great dangers as they imagine.

What the experience of Individual Psychology teaches is that a child should be told at the age of two that he is a boy or a girl. It should also be explained to him at that time that his sex can never be changed, and that boys grow up to be men and girls grow up to be women. If this is done, then the lack of other knowledge is not so dangerous. If it is brought home to him that a girl will not be educated like a boy nor a boy like a girl, then the sex role will be fixed in his mind and he will be sure to develop and to prepare for his role in a normal manner. If he believes, however, that through a certain trick he can change his sex, then trouble will result. Trouble will also result if the parents are always expressing a desire to change the sex of a child. In *The Well of Loneliness* we find an excellent literary presentation of this situation. Parents too often like to educate a girl like a boy or vice versa. They will photograph their children dressed in the clothes of the opposite sex. It sometimes happens, too, that a girl looks like a boy, and then people in the environment begin calling the child by its wrong sex. This may start a great confusion, which can very well be avoided.

There should also be avoided any discussion about the sexes which tends to undervalue the female sex, and to regard boys as superior. Children should be made to understand that both sexes are of equal worth. This is important not merely in order to prevent an inferiority complex on the part of the members of the undervalued sex, but also to prevent a bad effect upon the children of the male sex. If boys were not taught to think that they are the superior sex, they would not look upon girls as mere objects of desire. Nor would they look upon the relations of the sexes in an ugly light if they knew their future tasks.

In other words, the real problem of sex education is not merely explaining to children the physiology of sexual relationships—it involves the proper preparation of the whole attitude towards love and marriage. This is closely related to the question of social adjustment. If a person is not socially adjusted he will make a joke out of the question of sex and look at things entirely from the point of view of self-indulgence. This happens of course all too often, and is a reflex of the defects of our culture. Women have to suffer because under our culture it is much easier for a man to play the leading role. But the man also suffers because by means of this fictitious superiority he loses touch with the underlying values.

As regards the physical phase of sex education, it is not necessary that children receive this education very early in life. One can wait until the child becomes curious, until he wants to find out certain things. A mother and father who are interested in the child will also know when it is proper for them to take the lead if the child is too shy to ask questions. If he feels that his father and mother are comrades he will ask questions, and then the answers must be given in a manner proper to his understanding. One must avoid giving answers that stimulate the sex drive.

In this connection it may be said that one need not always be alarmed by apparently premature manifestations of the sex instinct. Sex development begins very early, in fact in the first weeks of life. It is wholly certain that an infant experiences erogenous pleasures, and that he sometimes seeks to stimulate the erogenous zones artificially. We should not be frightened if we see signs of the beginnings of certain nuisances, but we should do our best to put a stop to these practices without seeming to attach too much importance to them. If a child finds out that we are worried over these matters he will continue his habits deliberately in order to gain attention. It is such actions that make us think he is a victim of the sex drive, when he is really exploiting a habit as a tool for showing off. Generally little children try to gain attention by playing with their genital organs because they know that their parents are afraid of this practice. It is much the same psychology as when children play sick because they have noticed that when they are sick they are more pampered and more appreciated.

Children should not be stimulated bodily by too much kissing and embracing. It is cruel to the child, especially in the adolescent period. Nor should children be stimulated mentally on the subject of sex. It happens very often that a child will discover some frivolous pictures in the father's library. We hear constantly of such cases in the psychological clinics. The children should not be able to put their hands on books which deal with sexual matters on a plane above their age. Nor should they be taken to see moving picture shows in which the sex theme is exploited.

If one avoids all such forms of premature stimulation, one need not have any fears. One needs only to speak at the right time in a few simple words, never irritating the child and always giving answers in a true and simple manner. Above all one must never lie to the child, if one wants to retain his trust. If the child trusts the parent he will discount the explanations that he hears from his comrades—perhaps ninety per cent of mankind get their sexual knowledge from comrades—and will believe what the parent says. Such co-operation, such camaraderie is much more important than the various subterfuges that are used in the belief that they answer the situation.

THE EDUCATION OF CHILDREN

Children who experience too much of sex, or experience sex too early in life, generally shrink from sex later on. That is why it is a good thing to avoid having the children notice the love-making of parents. If possible they should not sleep in the same room—and certainly not in the same bed—with the parents. Also, sisters, and brothers should not sleep in the same room. The parents must keep an eye open to see that the children behave rightly, and they should also be on the watch for outside influences.

These remarks sum up the most important items in the matter of sex education. We see here, as in all other phases of education, the dominant importance of the sense of co-operation and friendliness within the family. With this co-operation present, and with an early knowledge of the sex role and of the equality of man and woman, the child is well prepared against any dangers that he may meet. And above all, he is well prepared for carrying on his work in a healthy manner.

CHAPTER THIRTEEN

PEDAGOGICAL MISTAKES

IN the rearing of children there are some things which the parent or teacher must never allow to discourage him. He must never grow hopeless because his efforts do not meet with immediate success; he must not anticipate defeat because the child is lethargic or apathetic or extremely passive; nor must he permit himself to be influenced by the superstition that there are gifted or ungifted children. Individual Psychology claims that the effort should be made with all children to stimulate their mental faculties by giving them more courage, more faith in themselves; by teaching them that difficulties are not to be regarded as insurmountable obstacles, but as problems to meet and conquer. Success will not always attend such efforts, but the many cases which are successful more than compensate for those which do not produce spectacular results. The following is an interesting case in which our efforts were successful:

This was the case of a twelve-year-old boy in his sixth year at elementary school. He had bad marks and was not in the least disturbed by them. He had an unusually infelicitous past history. He could not walk until he was about three years old on account of rickets. At the end of his third year he was able to speak only a few words. When he was four, his mother took him to a child psychologist who told her that the case was hopeless. The mother, however, did not believe this, and placed the child in a child guidance institute. There he developed slowly and without much help from the institute. When the boy was six it was decided that he was able to enter school. During the first two years at school, he received extra tutoring at home, so that he was able to pass his school examinations. He managed to get through the third class and through the fourth as well.

The situation at school and at home was as follows: The boy made himself noticeable at school by his great indolence; he complained that he did not seem able to concentrate and could not listen with attention. He did not get along well with his schoolmates, was teased by them and always showed himself weaker than the others. Among all his schoolmates he had only one friend whom he liked very much and with whom he went walking. He found the other children disagreeable and was unable to make contact with them. The teacher complained that the boy was weak in arithmetic and that he could not write; this in spite of the fact that the teacher was convinced that the boy was capable of accomplishing as much as the others.

In the light of the boy's past history and what he had already been able to do, it was clear that the treatment of the boy had been based on a mistaken diagnosis. Here was a child suffering from an intense feeling of inferiority—in short, an inferiority complex. The boy had an older brother who got along very well. His parents claimed that he was able to enter high school without ever studying. Parents like to say that their children do not have to study anything, and the children themselves then like to boast of it. It is evident that learning without some sort of studying is impossible. This older brother probably trained himself to do most of his studying in the classroom by listening intently and retaining what he heard and saw at school. Children who do not pay so much attention in school have to do their studying at home.

What a difference between the two boys! Our child had to live constantly under the oppressive feeling that he was less capable than his brother, and that he was worth infinitely less than he. He probably heard this often enough from his mother when she was angry with him, or from his brother who used to call him a fool or an idiot. His mother said that the older brother often kicked the younger when the latter did not obey him. We had the result before us: a human being who believed that he was worth less than others. Life seemed to confirm his belief. His schoolmates laughed at him; his school work was always faulty; he said he could not concentrate. Every difficulty frightened him. His teacher remarked from time to time that the child did not belong in that class or in that school. It is no wonder that the child finally believed that it was impossible to avoid the situation into which he had fallen, and he was convinced that the opinion which others had of him was correct. It is pathetic when a child is so discouraged that he has no faith in the future.

It was easy to see that this child had lost his faith, not because he trembled and grew pale when we began to chat with him in a cheery fashion, but from a small sign which should always be noted. When we asked him how old he was (we knew that he was twelve) he answered: "Eleven years." One should never take such an answer to be an accident since most children know exactly how old they are. We have often had occasion to ascertain that such mistakes have underlying reasons. When we consider what has happened in the life of this child, and then remember his answer, we get the impression that he is trying to recapture his past. He wants to return to the past, to the time when he was smaller, weaker and more in need of help than he is now.

We can reconstruct his system from the facts already at our disposal. This child does not seek his salvation in the accomplishment of those tasks usually given to a child of his age; but he believes and behaves as if he were not as fully developed as others and could not compete with them. This state of feeling himself behind the others is expressed in the reduction of his years. It is possible that he answers "eleven years" and behaves, under certain circumstances, like a child of five. He is so convinced of his inferiority that he attempts to adjust all his activities to this supposed state of being backward.

The child still wet himself in the daytime and he was unable to control his bowel movements. These are symptoms which appear when a child believes or wants to believe that he is still a baby. They confirm our statement that this boy wanted to cling to the past, and to return to it if possible.

There was a governess in the house who had been there before the child was born. She was very much attached to the child, and took the mother's place whenever possible, acting as the child's support. We could draw further conclusions. We already know how the boy lived, we know that he did not like to get up early in the morning. A description of how long it took him to arise was given us with a gesture of disgust. Our conclusion was that the boy did not like to go to school. A boy who does not get along with his schoolmates, who feels himself oppressed, who does not believe that he is capable of accomplishing anything, cannot possibly want to go to school. As a result, he will not want to get up in time for school.

His governess, however, said that he did want to go to school. In fact when he was sick recently he begged to be allowed to get up. This does not contradict in the least what we said. The question to be answered is, "How can the governess make such a mistake?" The circumstances were clear and amusing. When the boy was sick, he could permit himself to say that he wanted to go to school, since he knew positively that his governess would reply, "You cannot go because you are sick." His family, however, did not understand the seeming contradiction, and they were confused in their attempts to do something with the boy. We also had frequent opportunities to observe that the governess was incapable of understanding what was actually going on in the boy's mind.

Something else had developed which was the immediate cause of bringing the boy to us. He had taken money from the governess to buy candy. That also meant that he was behaving like a small child. To take money for candy is extremely childish. Very young children carry on in this fashion when they cannot control their greed for candy; they are the children who also cannot control their bodily functions. The psychological significance of this is: "You must watch me, otherwise I am capable of doing something naughty." The boy tried constantly to arrange situations which would make others occupy themselves with him because he had no confidence in himself. When we compared his situation at home and at school, the connection was clear. At home he could get people to occupy themselves with him; in school he could not. But who attempted to do something to correct the child's conduct?

Up to the time the boy was brought to us he was regarded as a backward, inferior child, and he did not in the least deserve this classification. He was a completely normal child who could accomplish as much as any of his schoolmates as soon as he regained faith in himself. He had always been inclined to view everything pessimistically, to accept defeat before he had made one step forward. His lack of self-confidence was expressed in every gesture and was confirmed in his teacher's report: "Cannot concentrate; weak memory; inattentive; has no friends; etc." His discouragement was so patent that no one would overlook it and circumstances were so much against him that it would have been difficult to change his point of view.

After our Individual Psychological questionnaire had been filled out the consultation followed. We had to confer not only with the boy but with a whole group of persons. First, the mother, who had long since given him up as hopeless and only tried to keep him going so that he would eventually be able to do some sort of work. Second, the older brother, who looked upon the younger boy with contempt.

Our boy naturally had no answer to the question, "What do you want to be when you grow up?" This is unusually characteristic. It is always suspicious when a half-grown child really does not know what he wants to become. It is true that people do not generally land in the profession they chose as children, but that does not matter. They are, at least, led by an idea. In their earliest years children want to become chauffeurs, watchmen, conductors, or whatever positions visible to them appear attractive to their childish valuations. But when a child has no material goal in view, it is to be suspected that he wants to keep his eyes away from the future, to return to the past; or, in other words, to avoid the future and all problems connected with it.

This seems to contradict one of the basic claims of Individual Psychology. We have always spoken of the striving for superiority characteristic of children, and we have attempted to show that every child wants to unfold himself, to become bigger than the others, to accomplish something. Suddenly we have before us a child of whom the contrary can be said; a child who wants to go backwards, wants to be small and to have others support him. How are we to explain it? Movements in mental life are not primitive. They have a complicated background. Were we to draw naïve conclusions in complicated cases we would always be mistaken. There are tricks in all these complications, and any dialectical attempt to make the opposite out of the thing itself, as, for example, to say that the boy struggles in a backward direction because he appears, in that way, the biggest, and in the safest position, must be confusing unless one understands the whole picture completely. In point of fact, these children are right in an amusing way. They can never be so strong or so dominating as during the time when they are really quite small, weak and helpless, and nothing is demanded of them. This child, who had no confidence in himself, was afraid he could not accomplish anything. Are we then to assume that he will willingly face a future which will expect something from him? He must avoid every situation in which his strength and abilities will be used to measure him as an individual. Nothing remains, therefore, but a greatly restricted sphere of activity where little will be asked of him. In this way we can understand that only a small portion remains of his striving for recognition, the recognition which he received as a tiny child dependent upon others.

We had to confer not only with the boy's teacher, his mother and older brother, but with his father and with our colleagues. Such a string of conferences entails much work, and a great deal of labor could be saved if we could win the teacher over. This is not impossible, but it is not simple. Many teachers still cling fast to old methods and beliefs and regard psychological examinations as something extraordinary. Many of them fear that a psychological examination indicates a loss of power or else they regard it as an unwarranted interference. This is, of course, not so. Psychology is a science which cannot be learned all at once, but must be studied and practiced. It is, however, of little use when one has the wrong point of view.

Tolerance is also a necessary quality, especially for a teacher, and it is wise to have an open mind to new psychological ideas, even when they seem to contradict the views we have held hitherto. As conditions exist to-day, we have no right to contradict flatly the opinion of the teacher. What are we to do in such a difficult situation? In our experience nothing remains to be done in such cases but to take the child out of his difficult predicament—that is to say, to remove him from that particular school. No one is hurt by this procedure. Practically no one knows what is going on, but a burden falls from the shoulders of the boy. He enters a new situation where nothing is known to him. He can take care not to let other people think badly of him, not to let himself be held in contempt by others. How this is arranged is not easy to explain. Family circumstances have a great deal to do with it. Probably every case requires a slightly different handling. It will, however, be much easier to deal with such children when there are a goodly number of teachers versed in Individual Psychology, who will regard such cases with understanding eyes and be able to help the children in the school.

CHAPTER FOURTEEN

EDUCATING THE PARENT

THIS book, as we have indicated on several occasions, is addressed to parents and teachers, both of whom may profit equally from the new psychological insight into the mental life of the child. In the last analysis, it does not matter much whether the education and development of the child take place for the most part under the auspices of the parent or under the auspices of the teacher, provided the child gets the proper education. We are referring of course to extra-curricular education—not the teaching of subjects of study, but the development of personality, which is the most important part of education. Now, although both the parent and the teacher can each contribute his share in this educational work—the parent correcting the deficiencies of the school, and the teacher correcting the deficiencies of the home—it is nonetheless true that in our large cities, and under modern social and economic conditions, the greater part of the responsibility falls on the teacher. Taken *en masse* parents are not as permeable to new ideas as are our teachers, who have a professional interest in the education of children. The hope of Individual Psychology in preparing the children of to-morrow rests primarily on converting the schools and the teachers—although the co-operation of parents is of course never rejected.

Now in the course of the educational work of the teacher, there comes up inevitably a conflict with the parent. The conflict is all the more inevitable in that the teacher's correctional work presupposes in some measure the failure of the parent. It is in a sense an accusation against the parent, and the parent very often feels it as such. How shall the teacher handle the parent in this type of situation?

The following remarks are addressed to this problem. They are written, of course, from the point of view of the teacher, who needs to handle the parent as a psychological problem. If these remarks are read by parents, they need give no offense, since they apply only to the unintelligent parent who forms the mass phenomenon that the teacher has to deal with.

Many a teacher has remarked that it is often more difficult to approach the parents of a problem child than it is to approach the child himself. This fact indicates that it is always necessary for the teacher to proceed with a certain amount of tact. The teacher must always act on the assumption that the parents are not responsible for all the bad qualities the child shows. The parents are after all not skillful pedagogues and they usually have only tradition to guide them. When they are summoned to school on account of their children they come feeling like accused criminals. Such a mood, bespeaking as it does some inward consciousness of guilt, demands the most tactful treatment at the hands of the teacher. It is therefore most desirable that the teacher should try in such cases to change the parents' mood to a friendly and a freer one, to place himself at the disposal of the parents as an assistant and to rely on their good intentions.

The parents should never be reproached even when there are just grounds. We can achieve much more when we succeed in establishing a sort of pact, when we persuade the parents to change their attitude and work with us according to our methods. It is of no avail to point out to them the faults in their past treatment. What we must do is to try to make them adopt a new procedure. To tell them that they have done this or that wrongly, only offends them and makes them unwilling to co-operate. As a rule the deterioration of a child does not take place out of a clear sky; there is always a past history. The parents come to school in the belief that they have overlooked something. They should never be permitted to feel that we think so; they should never be spoken to categorically or dogmatically. Suggestions to parents should never be made in an authoritative manner. The sentences should always have a "perhaps," "probably," "possibly," "you might try it this way." Even if we know exactly where the mistake is and how it is to be corrected, we should never point it out to the parents bluntly as if we want to force them. It goes without saying that so much tact is not always to be found in every teacher, neither is it acquired suddenly. It is interesting to see the same thoughts expressed in the autobiography of Benjamin Franklin. He writes there:

"A Quaker friend having kindly informed me that I was generally thought proud, that my pride showed itself frequently in conversation, that I was not content with being in the right when discussing any point, but was overbearing and rather insolent, of which he convinced me by mentioning several instances, I determined endeavoring to cure myself, if I could, of this vice or folly among the rest, and I added Humility to my list, giving an extensive meaning to the word.

"I cannot boast of much success in acquiring the *reality* of this virtue, but I had a good deal with regard to the *appearance* of it. I made it a rule to forbear all direct contradiction to the sentiments of others, and all positive assertion of my own. I even forbid myself, agreeably to the old laws of our Junto, the use of every word or expression in the language that imported a fixed opinion, such as certainly, undoubtedly, etc., and I adopted, instead of them, I conceive, I apprehend or I imagine a thing to be so or so, or so it appears to me at present. When another asserted something that I thought an error, I denied myself the pleasure of contradicting him abruptly and of showing immediately some absurdity in his proposition; and in answering I began by observing that in certain cases or circumstances his opinion would be right, but in the present case there appeared or seemed to me some difference, etc. I soon found the advantage of this change in my manner; the conversations I engaged in went on more pleasantly. The modest way in which I proposed my opinions procured them a readier reception and less contradiction; I had less mortification when I was found to be in the wrong, and I more easily prevailed with others to give up their mistakes and join with me when I happened to be in the right.

"And this mode, which I at first put on with some violence to natural inclination, became at length so easy, and so habitual to me, that perhaps for these fifty years past no one has ever heard a dogmatical expression escape me. And to this habit (after my character of integrity) I think it principally owing that I had early so much weight with my fellow-citizens when I proposed new institutions, or alterations in the old, and so much influence in public councils when I became a member; for I was but a bad speaker, never eloquent, subject to much hesitation in my choice of words, hardly correct in language, and yet I generally carried my points.

"In reality, there is, perhaps, no one of our natural passions so hard to subdue as pride. Disguise it, struggle with it, beat it down, stifle it, mortify it as much as one pleases, it is still alive, and will every now and then peep out and show itself; you will see it, perhaps, often in this history; for, even if I could conceive that I had completely overcome it, I should probably be proud of my humility."

It is true that these words do not fit every situation in life. This can neither be expected nor demanded. Franklin's attitude, nevertheless, shows us how unsuitable and unsuccessful aggressive opposition may be. There is no basic law in life which holds good for every situation. Every rule goes only so far and then all of a sudden becomes unworkable. There are certainly situations in which a strong word is the only right one. However, when we consider the situation between the teacher on the one hand, and, on the other, the worried parents who have already experienced humiliation and are prepared for further humiliation on account of their child, and when we also consider that without the parents' co-operation we can do nothing, it is obvious that Franklin's method is the only logical one to adopt in order to help the child.

Under such circumstances, where it is of no importance to be able to prove that one is right, or to show one's superiority, but where it is necessary to prepare the road which we must tread to help the child, there are naturally many difficulties. Many parents do not want to hear any suggestions. They are astonished or indignant, impatient and inimical because the teacher has placed them and their child in such an unpleasant situation. Such parents have usually been trying for some time to close their eyes to the faults of their child, to blind themselves to reality. Suddenly their eyes are forcibly opened for them. The whole matter is most disagreeable, and it is understandable that a teacher who approaches such parents brusquely or too energetically loses all possibility of winning the parents over to his side. Many parents go even further. They meet the teacher with a verbal tide of indignation and make themselves unapproachable. In such cases it is better to show the parents that the teacher is dependent upon their assistance; it is better to quiet them and bring them to the point of speaking in a friendly manner with the teacher. It must not be forgotten that parents are often so entangled in the meshes of traditional, antiquated methods that they cannot free themselves quickly.

For example, when a father has discouraged his child badly by stern words and a sour facial expression, it is naturally hard for him, after ten years, suddenly to assume a friendly expression and to speak kindly to the child. It might be mentioned here that when a father suddenly changes his whole attitude towards his child, the latter will not believe at first that the change is a sincere one. He will regard it as a trick and will have to gain confidence slowly in his parent's changed demeanor. Highly intellectual persons are no exceptions. There is a case of a high school principal who had driven his son almost to the point of breakdown by constant criticising and nagging. The principal realized this in a conversation he had with us; then he went home and delivered a scathing sermon to his son. He had lost his temper again because his son had been lazy. Every time his son did something which did not please him his father lost his temper and spoke cruelly. When this is possible with a man who considers himself a pedagogue we can imagine how it is with those parents who have grown up with the dogmatic idea that every child must be punished for his mistakes by a whipping. Every device known to diplomatic art, every tactful phrase which occurs to the teacher must be employed in conversations with parents.

It must not be forgotten that the custom of educating children to the accompaniment of blows is widely spread in the poorer classes. And so it happens that children from these ranks, going home after a corrective conference with their teacher, find a continuation in the form of a whipping awaiting them from their parents. We are in the sad state of having to remember that our pedagogical efforts are all too frequently brought to naught by the unwise parental treatment at home. In such cases, children are often punished twice for the same mistake, when we are of the opinion that once is enough.

We know the terrible results which sometimes follow such double punishment. Take the case of a child who must bring home a bad report card. Afraid of a whipping, he does not show it to his parents, and then afraid of punishment at school, he plays truant; or else he forges his parent's signature to the card. We must not overlook these facts, nor must we regard them lightly; we must always regard the child in his relation to the various elements in his environment. We must ask ourselves: What happens now when I go ahead. How will it affect this child. What certainty have I that it will have a beneficial effect on him? Has the child gotten to the point where he can bear a burden, and will he be able to learn something constructive from it?

We know how differently children and adults react to difficulties. We must be most careful in re-education and must be reasonably certain of results before we attempt to remould the life pattern of a child. He who has always proceeded with deliberation and objective judgment in the education and re-education of children will be able to predict with greater certainty the results of his efforts. Practice and courage are essential in pedagogical work, as is also the unshakable belief that no matter what the circumstances may be, there is always a way to prevent a child from having a breakdown. First of all, there is the old and well-recognized rule that it is never too early to start. He who is accustomed to regard a human being as a unity and to regard symptoms as part of a unity, will be able to understand and to help a child very much better than he who is accustomed to seize upon a symptom and treat it according to some rigid scheme—as in the case, say, of a teacher who, when a child has failed to do his homework, immediately writes a note about it to the child's parents.

We are entering a period which is bringing with it new ideas, new methods and new understanding in the education of children. Science is doing away with old worn out customs and traditions. The knowledge we are gaining places more responsibility on the teacher, but as a compensation it gives him far more understanding of the problems of childhood and with it far greater ability to help the children who pass through his hands. The important thing to remember is that a single conduct manifestation has no meaning when detached from the personality as a whole, and that we can understand it only when we study it in connection with the rest of the human being.

AN INDIVIDUAL PSYCHOLOGICAL
QUESTIONNAIRE

For the Understanding and Treatment of Problem-
Children, Drawn up by the International
Society of Individual Psychologists.

1. Since when has there been cause for complaint? What sort of situation (psychic or otherwise) did the child find himself in when his failings
were first noticed?

> The following are important: change of en-
> vironment, beginning of school life, births in
> the family, younger or older brothers and sis-
> ters, failures in school, changes of teachers or
> school, new friendships, illnesses of the child,
> divorce, new marriage, death of the parents.

2. Were any peculiarities noticed at an earlier
age in regard to mental or physical weakness, timidity, carelessness, reserve, clumsiness, envy, jealousy, dependence on others when eating, dressing,
washing or going to bed? Was the child afraid of

being alone or of darkness? Does he understand his sexual role? Any primary, secondary or tertiary characteristics of gender? How does he regard the opposite sex? How far has he been enlightened on his sexual role? Is he a stepchild? Illegitimate? A foster child? Orphan? How did his foster parents treat him? Is there still a contact? Did he learn to speak and walk at the right time? Without difficulty? Was the teething normal? Noticeable difficulties in learning to read, draw, sing, swim? Is he particularly attached to either his father, his mother, his grandparents or his nurse?

> It is necessary to determine whether he is hostile towards his environment, and to look for the origin of his feeling of inferiority; whether there is a tendency to avoid difficulties and whether he shows traits of egoism and sensitiveness.

3. Does the child give much trouble? What and whom does he fear most? Does he cry out at night? Does he suffer from enuresis? Is he domineering towards weaker children or towards stronger children as well? Did he show a strong desire to sleep in his parents' bed? Was he clumsy? Did he suffer from rickets? What about his intelligence? Was he much teased and derided? Does he show vanity in regard to his hair, clothes, shoes, etc.? Does he in-

THE EDUCATION OF CHILDREN

dulge in nail-biting or nose-picking? Is he greedy
when eating?

> It would be illuminating to know if he strives
> more or less courageously after priority; fur-
> ther, if obstinacy prevents him from pursuing
> his impulse to action.

4. Does he make friends easily? Does he show tolerance towards persons and animals, or does he
molest and torment them? Is he fond of collecting or
hoarding? What about avarice and covetousness?
Does he lead others? Is he inclined to isolate himself?

> These questions are in connection with the
> child's ability to "get in touch" and the degree
> of his discouragement.

5. With reference to all the above questions, what
is the present position of the child? How does he conduct himself in school? Does he like school? Is he
punctual? Is he excited before going to school? Is
he in a hurry? Does he lose his books, satchel,
exercise-books? Is he excited about exercises and
before examinations? Does he forget to do his school
work, or does he refuse to do it? Does he waste his
time? Is he lazy? Is there a lack of concentration?
Does he disturb the class? How does he regard the
teacher? Is he critical, arrogant, indifferent towards

253

the teacher? Does he ask others to help him with his lessons or does he wait until he is invited? Is he ambitious in regard to gymnastics and sport? Does he consider himself comparatively untalented or entirely so? Is he a great reader? What sort of literature does he prefer?

> Questions that help us to understand how far the child is properly prepared for school life, the result of the "going to school experiment," and his attitude towards difficulties.

6. Correct information about home circumstances, illness in the family, alcoholism, criminal tendencies, neurosis, debility, lues, epilepsy, the standard of living. Any deaths in the family, and how old was the child when they occurred? Is he an orphan? Who is the dominating spirit of the family? Is the home education strict, with much grumbling and fault-finding, or is it indulgent? Are the home influences such as to make the child afraid of life? What about supervision?

> From his position and attitude in the family circle we may judge of the impressions the child receives.

7. What is the child's position in regard to his place in the family constellation? Is he the eldest, the youngest, the only child, the only boy, the only

girl? Is there rivalry, much crying, malicious laughter, a strong tendency to depreciate others?

> The above is important for the study of character, and throws light on the child's attitude towards others.

8. Has the child formed any ideas about the choice of a profession? What does he think about marriage? What profession do the other members of the family follow? What about the married life of the parents?

> It may be concluded from this whether the child has courage and confidence for the future.

9. What are his favorite games, stories, characters in history and fiction? Is he fond of spoiling other children's games? Is he imaginative? Is he a cool-headed thinker? Does he indulge in daydreaming?

> These questions are in reference to a possible tendency to play the hero in life. A contrast in the child's behavior may be regarded as a sign of discouragement.

10. Earliest remembrances? Impressive or periodical dreams about flying, falling, powerlessness, late arrival at railway station, anxiety dreams?

> In this connection we often find a tendency to isolation, warnings to be careful, ambitious traits and a preference for particular persons, country life, etc.

255

11. In what respect is the child discouraged? Does he consider himself neglected? Does he respond readily to attention and praise? Has he superstitious ideas? Does he avoid difficulties? Does he try his hand at various things only to give them up again? Is he uncertain about his future? Does he believe in the injurious effects of heredity? Was he systematically discouraged by those around him? Is his outlook on life pessimistic?

> Answers to these questions will help us to prove that the child has lost confidence in himself and that he is now on the wrong road.

12. Are there other tricks and bad habits, e. g., grimacing, pretending to be stupid, childish, comical?

> In such cases slight courage is manifested for the purpose of attracting attention.

13. Has he speech disabilities? Is he ugly? Club-footed? Knock-kneed or bow-legged? Stunted? Abnormally stout or tall? Badly proportioned? Has he constitutional abnormalities of eye or ear? Is he mentally backward? Left-handed? Does he snore at night? Is he remarkably handsome?

> These are disadvantages which the child as a rule overestimates, and by which he may be permanently discouraged. A faulty develop-

ment is often seen too in the case of very pretty children who become obsessed with the idea that they should get everything they want without exerting themselves. Such children miss numerous opportunities of preparing themselves for life.

14. Does he often talk of his incapacity, his "lack of talent" for school, for work, for life? Does he harbor suicidal thoughts? Is there any connection in point of time between his failures and troubles? Does he overrate apparent success? Is he servile, bigoted, rebellious?

> Here we have manifestations of extreme discouragement, mostly apparent after vain efforts on the part of the child to get rid of his troubles. His failures are due partly to the ineffectuality of his efforts and partly to a lack of understanding of persons in touch with him. But his inclinations must be satisfied somehow, somewhere; so he seeks some other, easier scene of action. "Nebenkriegsschauplatz."

15. Name the things in which the child is successful.

> Such "positive performances" give us important hints, for it is possible that the interests, inclinations and preparations of the child point in a different direction from that in which he has hitherto gone.

From answers to the above questions (which

THE EDUCATION OF CHILDREN

should never be put in regular sequence or routine-like, but constructively and by way of conversation) a correct notion of the individuality is formed. It will be seen that though the failures are not justified, they are conceivable and can be understood. The errors disclosed should always be explained in a patient and friendly way, without any threats.

FIVE CASE HISTORIES WITH COMMENTARIES

I

A boy, fifteen years old, is the only child of parents who have worked hard to achieve a modestly comfortable existence. They have been careful to see that the boy had everything necessary for physical health. In his early years the boy was happy and healthy. His mother is a good woman, but she cries too easily. Her report of her son is made with much effort and many interruptions. We do not know the father, but the mother describes him as an honest, energetic man who loves his family and who has much confidence in himself. When the boy was very young and was disobedient, the father would remark, "It would be a fine state of affairs if I couldn't break his will." His idea of "breaking" was setting the boy a good example, not bothering to teach him much, but whipping him whenever he did something

wrong. In the boy's early childhood, his rebellious-
ness was expressed by his wanting to play master of
the house, a desire frequently found in the spoiled,
only child. He showed early a striking inclination to
disobedience and developed the habit of refusing
to obey so long as he did not feel the hand of his
father.

When we stop here and ask what salient character trait will surely develop in this child, we must
answer, "Lying." He will lie to escape his father's
heavy hand. It is indeed the chief complaint with
which the mother comes to us. To-day the child is
fifteen years old and the parents never know whether
he is lying or telling the truth. When we probe a little more deeply, we hear the following: The child
was for a time in a parochial school, where his
teachers also complained that he was disobedient and
disturbed the class. For example, he would shout the
answer to a question before he was asked, or he would
ask a question in order to interrupt, or talk loudly to
his classmates during class. He would write his
homework in a most illegible hand—he was, moreover, left-handed. His conduct finally got beyond all
bounds and his lying was noticeable as soon as he
feared punishment from his father. His parents at

first decided to leave him in the school, but before long they had to take him out because his teacher concluded that nothing could be done with him.

The boy looked like a lively lad whose intelligence was recognized by all the teachers. He finished public school and had to take the entrance examinations for high school. His mother awaited him after the examination and he told her that he had passed the test. Every one was very happy and they all went to the country for the summer. The boy frequently spoke of high school. Then the high school reopened. The boy packed his schoolbag, went to school and came home each day for lunch. One day, however, the mother walked with him part of the way and as they crossed the street together, she heard a man say, "There's the boy who showed me the way to the station this morning." His mother asked him what the man meant, and whether he hadn't been to school that morning. The lad answered that school had ended at ten o'clock, and he had walked with the man to the railroad station. His mother was not satisfied with the explanation and later spoke to the father about the matter. The father decided to accompany his son to school the following day. The next day, on the way to school, the father learned, in answer to his insistent questioning, that the boy had failed in his entrance examinations, that he had never been to high school, and that he had loafed around the streets all these days.

His parents engaged a tutor and the boy was eventually able to pass the examinations, but his conduct did not improve. He still disturbed the classroom procedure, and one day he began to steal. He stole some money from his mother, lied violently about it, and only confessed when threatened with the police. And now we have before us a case of sad neglect. The father, whose pride was such that he thought he could bend this twig, now gives his son up as hopeless. The boy is punished by being left alone with no one speaking to him or paying any attention to him. His parents also claim that they no longer beat him.

In answer to the question "Since when has there been cause for complaint?" the mother replies, "Since his birth." When we receive such an answer, we assume that the mother wants to imply that the boy's bad conduct is inborn, since his parents have tried everything to straighten him out, and have been unsuccessful.

THE EDUCATION OF CHILDREN

As a baby, the boy was extremely restless, he cried day and night. All the doctors, however, declared that he was quite normal and healthy.

This is not as simple as it sounds. There is nothing remarkable in the fact that nursing infants cry. There are many reasons for it, especially in the case of an only child where the mother has had no previous experience. Such children usually cry when they are wet, a condition of which the mother is not always aware. What did his mother do when he cried? She took the baby in her arms, rocked it and gave it something to drink. What she should have done was to find out the real cause of the crying, make the child comfortable and then pay no more attention to him. The child would have stopped crying and would not now have this black spot in his past.

His mother says that he learned to talk and walk at a normal age without difficulty, and that his teeth developed normally. He had a habit of destroying his playthings soon after they were given to him. Such manifestations are often found without necessarily indicating a bad character. Worthy of note is the sentence, "It was impossible to make him occupy himself for any length of time with any one thing." We must ask here how should a mother train a child to play alone. There is only one way to do it. The child must be permitted to occupy himself without constant interruption by adults. We suspect that this mother did not do this and several remarks indicate it; for example, that the boy always gave her a lot to do, that he always clung to her, etc. Here are the child's first attempts to induce his mother to pamper him, the oldest inscriptions on the scroll of his soul.

The child was never left alone.
The mother obviously says that in self-defense.

He was never alone and to this day he does not like to be left alone even for an hour. Evenings he is never alone, and he has also never been left alone during the night hours.
Here is proof of how closely the child is tied to his mother and how he has always been able to lean on her.

He was never afraid, and does not know fear today.
That is a statement which challenges psychological common sense since it does not agree with our findings. A closer examination of the facts gives us the explanation. The boy has never been left alone;

there was, therefore, no necessity for him to be afraid, since with such children fear is a means to compel others to remain with them. Consequently there was no place for fear, an emotion which he would have manifested as soon as he was left alone. Now comes another seeming contradiction.

He has a great fear of his father's cane. So he did have fear? *When the whipping was over, however, he forgot it quickly and was lively again, even though he was sometimes spanked severely.*

Here we see the unfortunate contrast: the mother yielding; the father stern, wanting to correct the mother's softness. And the child is driven more and more in the direction of his mother through his father's harshness. That is to say, he turns toward the person who pampers him, toward the person from whom he can get everything easily and cheaply.

In the parochial school, at the age of six, he came under the supervision of the priests, and at that time the complaints began about his liveliness, restlessness and inattentiveness. Complaints about his conduct were much more frequent than about his schoolwork. What was most noticeable was his restlessness. When a child wants to attract attention what better method can he choose than to be restless? This

THE EDUCATION OF CHILDREN

child wants to be noticed. He has formed the habit of attracting his mother's attention, and now, in a larger circle, he wants the attention of the new members of the larger group at school. When the teacher does not understand the child's purpose, he attempts to correct the child's conduct by singling him out for scolding or for reprimanding, and the boy is then where he wants to be. He has to pay a big price for the attention he secures, but he is used to that. He received enough beatings at home and remained unchanged. Are we to assume that he is to be dislodged from his old ways by the milder forms of punishment permitted the school? That is most improbable. When he condescended to go to school, he wanted to be the center of attention as a compensation.

The parents tried to improve his behavior by pointing out to him that it was necessary for the good of the class that every one keep quiet. When one hears such antiquated admonitions, one is somewhat dubious about the common sense of the parents. The boy knows as well as the grown-ups what is right and what is wrong. He is, however, busy with quite another problem. He wants to be noticed and he cannot gain any attention in school by being quiet; neither is it easy to gain attention by hard work. We see no riddle in his conduct as soon as we are aware of the task he has set himself. Obviously, when the father comes along with his cane, the boy will be quiet for a while. But the mother says that as soon as the father goes away, the boy starts all over again. He regards the whippings and punishments only as interruptions which disturb his progress for short periods, but do not by any means achieve the effect of permanent change.

But his temperament always broke through the restraint.

Children who want to attract attention must obviously do it by temperament. We see that what one usually calls temperament is nothing more than a convenient rhythm in which one fulfills tasks and is a form of movement determined by the goal. For example, if one wants to lie quietly on the sofa one will not need to develop such temperament. This temperament becomes a suspicious indication of what a person has in mind—in our case, to make himself conspicuous.

He formed the habit of taking all sorts of things from the house to school, exchanging them for money and entertaining his comrades with the proceeds. When his parents discovered this he was searched each day before leaving for school. He finally abandoned the practice and confined himself to playing jokes and making interruptions. This change was brought about only by severe punishment from his father.

We can understand his playing jokes; that belongs to his desire to make others notice him, to force his teacher to penalize him and to make himself superior to the school regulations.

His attempts to create disturbances gradually diminished, but returned periodically in full force and resulted in his being expelled from one school.

Here is the confirmation of what we said before. This boy, who struggles to obtain recognition from others, naturally meets obstacles and becomes aware of them. In addition, when we consider that he was left-handed, we have more insight into his mind. We can deduce that although he wanted to avoid difficulties, he always managed to find them and then lacked confidence to tackle them. But the less confidence he had in himself the more he wanted to demonstrate that he was worthy of attention. He did not cease his mischief-making until the school could no longer tolerate him and expelled him. When one has the justifiable standpoint that the school cannot permit one sinner to disturb the work of all the other students, there remains nothing else to do but expel the sinner. However, when we believe that the purpose of education is to correct shortcomings, expulsion is not the right method. It made it easier for the boy to obtain recognition from his mother, and he no longer had to exert himself in school.

It is to be noted here that he was, on the advice of one teacher, sent to a home during the vacation period. There he was under more strict supervision than even at school and this experiment was also a failure. His parents, however, were still the chief supervisors. The child went home every Sunday—a fact which pleased him very much. Yet, when he was not allowed to go home, he did not sulk. This is understandable. He wanted to play the great man and be regarded as such by others. He made no fuss about a whipping, did not permit himself to cry, nor in any way to behave in an unmanly fashion, no matter how disagreeable things were.

His school report cards were never very bad; he always had tutoring at home.

We conclude from this, that he was not independent. The parents were told by the teacher that the boy could learn very much better if only he were somewhat quieter. We are convinced that the boy can learn since there are no children, apart from the feeble-minded, who cannot learn.

He has no talent for drawing.

This is important since it may be assumed from the statement that he has not entirely overcome the clumsiness of his right hand.

He is one of the best in the gymnasium; he learned to swim quickly and has no fear of danger.

That shows that he is not completely discouraged, but that he has been using his courage for unimportant things—for those things which he could do easily and in which he was sure of success.

He is a stranger to shyness and tells every one what he thinks, no matter whether it happens to be the janitor or director of the school, in spite of the fact that he has been admonished time and again not to be forward.

We already know that he pays no attention when he is forbidden to do this or that, and we cannot therefore accept his lack of shyness as evidence of courage. We know that many children are well aware of the distance that separates them from the teachers and officials of the school. This boy who is not afraid of being whipped by his father, is naturally not afraid of the principal and speaks impudently in order to make himself important, and in this way he actually achieves his goal.

He is not quite certain about his sex, but says frequently that he wouldn't like to be a girl.

There are no definite indications as to his opinion of his own sex, but we always find in boys of such mischievous character the tendency to degrade girls. They derive a sense of their own superiority from the degradation of the girls.

He has no real friends.

This is quite understandable, since other children do not always like to give him the role of leader.

His parents have not explained sex matters to him as yet. His behavior is always an expression of a desire to rule.

He himself knows the facts which we have to get about him with so much effort. That is to say, he knows well what he wants, but he unquestionably does not know the connection between his unconscious goal and his behavior. He does not understand the extent and origin of this intense desire to rule. He wants to rule because he sees his father ruling, and the more he wants to rule, the weaker he really is, because he has to depend upon others; while his father, whom he has taken as a model, rules in a self-contained manner. In other words his ambition feeds on his weakness.

He always wants to start something, even with those stronger than he is.

These stronger persons are, however, weaker because they take their duties seriously. The boy only trusts himself when he can be impudent. Incidentally, it will not be easy to rid him of this impudence because he has no faith in his ability to learn anything and, therefore, has to hide behind this impudence.

He is not selfish, he gives freely.

If one were to assume this to be a sign of goodness, it would be difficult to find the connection with the rest of his character. We know that one can show superiority by being generous. It is important to see how this trait fits in with a lust for power. This generosity is felt by him as a personal elevation. It is probable that he has learned from his father this trick of showing off by being generous.

He still makes a lot of trouble. He is afraid first of all of his father, then of his mother. He is ready to get up at any hour and is not particularly vain.

This last concerns outer vanity, since his inner vanity is extraordinarily great.

He has given up the old habit of picking his nose. He is a stubborn child, fussy about food, does not like vegetables or fats. He is not completely uncompanionable, but prefers those children with whom he can do anything, and likes animals and flowers very much.

A liking for animals always has as a background a striving for superiority, a desire to rule. Such a liking is certainly not objectionable since it tends toward a union with all things earthly. With such children, however, we find that it expresses a wish to rule, and always tends to give the mother something more to attend to.

He manifested a great desire for leadership, to be sure not for intellectual leadership. He developed a tendency to collect things, but not possessing sufficient patience, no collection was ever completed.

The tragedy of such persons consists in the fact that they leave everything unfinished, because they are afraid of the responsibility of a completed result.

On the whole his behavior has improved since the age of ten. It was impossible formerly to keep him in the house since he always wanted to play the hero on the streets. His improvement has been brought about at the cost of great effort.

To confine him to the narrow limits of the house proved in reality the best means of satisfying his strong desire for self-assertion. Small wonder that he does more mischief within these narrow confines. He should have been left on the street under proper supervision.

When he comes home he turns to his school work, shows no desire for leaving the house, but finds ways for wasting his time.

We shall always be confronted with distraction and time-wasting when we confine a child to such a narrow sphere that he has always to work under supervision. He must be given an opportunity for activity—for joining other children so as to be able to play a role among his fellows.

THE EDUCATION OF CHILDREN

He used to go gladly to school.

This suggests that his teacher was not severe. In this way he was easily able to play the part of a hero.

He used to lose most of his school books. He was not afraid of examinations, he always believed that he could do everything brilliantly.

We find here a rather common trait. The fact that a given person is optimistic under all circumstances shows that he does not believe in himself. Such persons are certainly pessimists, but they manage to do violence to logic, taking refuge in a dream world where they can attain everything; they display no signs of surprise when they are confronted with defeat. They are possessed of a feeling of predestination enabling them to appear as optimists.

He suffers from a great lack of concentration. He is liked by some teachers and greatly disliked by others.

In any case he seems to be liked by the milder teachers who are pleased with his manners. He also disturbs them less, because no difficult tasks are assigned to him. Like most spoiled children, he lacks either the inclination or the habit of concentration. Up to the age of six he felt no need for this, since his mother took care of everything. Everything in life had been prearranged, as if he were enclosed in a cage. His lack of preparation made itself felt as soon as he was confronted with difficulties. He had acquired no means for meeting difficulties, he had no interest in others so as to be able to co-operate with them. He had neither the desire nor the self-confidence necessary to accomplish something independently. What he possessed was the desire for prominence—the desire to get to the front without any effort. But he failed to disturb the peace of the school—he failed to get attention, and this made his character worse.

He always wanted to take everything easily, and get everything in the easiest way without regard for other people. This had become the dominant motif of his life, which was expressed in all his specific acts, such as thefts and lies.

The mistake underlying the development of his life style is obvious. His mother, to be sure, supplied him with a stimulus for developing his social sentiments, but neither his mother nor his stern father succeeded in determining their further course. These sentiments were confined to the world of his mother. In his mother's presence he felt himself to be the center of attention.

THE EDUCATION OF CHILDREN

His striving for superiority was thus no longer directed towards the useful side of life but towards the vanity of his own person. In order to bring him to the useful side of life, the development of his character must be started anew. His confidence must be gained, so that he would gladly listen to us. At the same time we must widen the sphere of his social relations and in this way make good what the mother failed to do with the only child. He will have to be reconciled with his father. His education has to proceed step by step until the boy will be able to understand the mistake of his past life style in the same way that we understand it. Since his interest will no longer be focussed upon a single person, his independence and courage will grow and he will direct his superiority striving towards the useful side of life.

II

This is a case of a ten-year-old boy.

The complaint of the school is that his work is poor and that he is three terms behind.
Ten years old and three terms behind—we would suspect that he is feeble-minded.

He is now in 3B. His I. Q. is 101.

He therefore cannot be feeble-minded. What can be the cause of his backwardness? Why does he corrupt the class? We see a certain striving and a certain activity on his part, but all on the useless side. He wants to be creative, active and the center of attention, but in the wrong way. We can also see that he fights the school. He is a fighter. He is an enemy to the school, and, therefore, we understand why he should be backward, the routine of the school is very difficult for such a fighter.

He is slow to obey commands.

This is very obvious. He acts intelligently, that is to say, there is a method in his madness. If he is a fighter then he has to resist commands.

He fights with other boys; he brings toys to school.

He wants to make his own school.

He is bad in oral arithmetic.

This means that he lacks social-mindedness and the social logic that goes with it (See Chapter VII).

He has a speech defect and goes to a speech class once a week.

This speech defect is not based on an organic deficiency. This is a symptom of a lack of social co-operation, which shows itself in his impeded speech. Language is an attitude of co-operation—the individual has to connect himself with another person. As things are, the boy uses this speech defect as a tool for his combativeness. We need not wonder that he does not seek to remedy this speech defect, for to remedy it means to give up this tool with which he attracts attention.

When the teacher talks to him he moves his body from side to side.

It is as if he were preparing an attack. He does not enjoy having the teacher speak to him, because he is not the center of attention. The teacher is the conqueror if she speaks and he has to listen.

The mother (to be exact, the stepmother, since the mother died in his infancy) *only complains that he is nervous.*

This mysterious idea of nervousness covers a multitude of sins.

He was brought up by two grandmothers.

One grandmother is bad enough—we know that grandmothers usually pamper the children in a terrible way. It is worth while to consider why they do it. It is the fault of our culture—there is no place for older women. They rebel against this treatment and want to be treated rightly—wherein they are quite right. The grandmother wants to prove the importance of her existence and she does this by pampering the children and getting them to cling to her. In this way she asserts her right to be recognized as a personality.

If you hear that there are two grandmothers then you can understand that there is a terrible competition going on. One will want to prove that the children like her more than the other. Naturally, under this competition for its favor the child finds himself in a sort of paradise where he gets everything he wants. All he needs to say is, "The other grandmother gave me this," and the other will want to outbid her rival. At home this child is the center of attention, and we can see how he makes this attention his goal. Now he is in school where there are not two grandmothers—there is only one teacher and many children. The only way he can be the center of attention here is by fighting.

During the time he was living with the grandmothers he did not get good marks at school.

The school was not the right place for him. He was not prepared for it. The school was a test of his ability to co-operate, and he was not trained for it. A mother is the one who can best develop this ability for co-operation.

The father remarried a year and a half ago and the child lives with the father and stepmother.

Here we find, of course, a difficult situation. The trouble begins or the trouble is increased when a stepmother or stepfather enters into the situation. The problem of step-parents is traditional and it has not yet been improved; the child especially suffers. Stepmothers, even of the best kind, generally have trouble. One need not say that the problem of step-parents is insoluble, but it can be solved only in a certain manner. Stepmothers and stepfathers should not expect appreciation as their right, but they should try their best to win appreciation. With two grandmothers to complicate the situation, the difficulty of the stepmother with the child is increased.

The stepmother tried to be affectionate when she first came into the family. She did all she could to win the boy. An older brother is a problem also.

Another fighter in the family, and think of the terrible rivalry between the two brothers which only increases the general combativeness.

The child fears the father and obeys him, but he does not obey the mother. Therefore she reports him to the father.

This is really a confession that the mother cannot educate the child, and so she puts it up to the man. When the mother always reports to the father what the children do and do not do, when she menaces them with the words, "I will tell your father," the children understand that she is not able to manage them and has given up the job. So they look for occasions to boss her. When the mother speaks and acts in this way she expresses her inferiority complex.

Mother will take him out to places and buy him things if he promises to behave.

The mother is in a difficult situation. Why? Because the grandmother overshadows her, as the children think the grandmother is more important.

The grandmother sees him only occasionally.

It is very easy for a person who comes only for a

few hours to meddle with the children and leave all the trouble for the mother.

There does not seem to be any one in the family who really loves the child.
It appears that they do not like him any more. After spoiling him by pampering, even the grandmother now dislikes him.

The father whips him.
The whipping does not help, however. The child likes praise and if praised he is always wholly contented. But he does not know how to earn praise by acting in a right way. He prefers to demand praise from the teacher without earning it.

He works better if he receives praise.
This is of course the case with all children who want to be the center of attention.

Teachers do not like him because he is sullen.
This is the best means he could use, because he is a fighter.

The child suffers from enuresis.
This is also an expression of his desire to be the

283

center of attention. He is not fighting in a direct way but in an indirect way. How can such a child fight his mother in an indirect way? By wetting the bed and making her get up in the middle of the night; by screaming out in the night; by reading in bed instead of going to sleep; by not getting up in the morning; by bad eating habits. In short, he always has some means to occupy the mother with him, both in the daytime and at night. Enuresis and speech defect—with these two weapons he fights the environment.

The mother has tried to rid him of this habit by waking him several times in the night.

The mother is therefore with him several times in the night. Thus, even in this way he attains his goal.

Children are not fond of the boy because he wants to boss them. A few weak ones try to imitate him.

He is a weak and discouraged person, and does not want to carry on in a courageous manner. The weak children in the school like to imitate him because this is really the right way for weak children to gain attention.

On the other hand, he is not really disliked, and "the other children are glad to think that he has improved whenever his work is chosen as the best."

The children are glad when he improves. This is also a very good indication about the teacher. The teacher really understands how to make the co-operative spirit live in the children.

The boy likes to play ball on the street with other children.

He has relations with others when he is sure to succeed and conquer.

The case was discussed with the mother and it was explained to her that she was in a very difficult situation with the child and the grandmothers. It was also explained to her that the boy is jealous of the older brother and is always afraid that he may be left behind. During the interview the boy did not speak a word although he was told that we were all his friends at the clinic. Speech for this boy would mean co-operation. He wants to fight, and so instead of speaking he refrains from speaking. It is the same lack of social-mindedness which we saw expressed in his refusal to do anything about his speech defect.

This may seem astonishing, but it is a fact that

285

we very often find even adult persons who act this way in social life—they fight by not speaking. There was once a couple who had a violent quarrel. The husband screamed very loudly and said to his wife, "Just see, now you are silent!" She replied, "I am not silent, I only do not speak!"

In the case of this boy he, too, "only does not speak." When the interview was over he was told that he could go but he did not seem to want to leave. He was antagonized. He was told that the discussion was over and still he did not go. He was told to come again with the father next week.

In the meantime, we said to him. "You acted quite rightly not to speak since you always do the contrary thing. If you are told to speak, you are silent; when you should be silent in school, then you corrupt the class by your talking. You believe that in this way you are a hero. If we told you, 'Don't speak at all!' then you would speak. We only need to lead you on and ask the contrary of what we want."

The child obviously could be made to speak because it would be necessary for him to answer questions. In this way he would co-operate by speech and language. Later on the situation could be explained to him and he could be convinced of his mistakes, and in this way gradually improved.

In this connection, it should be borne in mind that so long as such a child is in his old accustomed situation he has no incentive to change. The mother, father, grandmothers, teachers, comrades—all fit into his accustomed life-style. His attitudes are fixed in respect to them. But when he comes to the clinic it is an altogether new situation that confronts him. We must even try to make this new situation as new as possible—a totally new environment in fact. He will better reveal the character traits belonging to the old situation to which he is trained. It is a good idea in such a case to tell him "you must not speak at all!" Whereupon he will say, "I will speak!" In this way nobody has entered into conversation with him directly, and he is not on guard with his inhibitions.

At the clinic, the children generally stand before a large audience, and this impresses them very much. It is a new situation and it gives the impression that they are not only not tied up with their own small environment but that others are also interested, and that they are thus a part of a larger whole. All this makes them want to be more a part of the whole than before, especially if they are asked to come again. They know what will happen

—they will be questioned and asked how they are getting on, etc. Some come once a week and some come every day depending on the nature of the case. They are trained for their behavior toward the teacher. They know that they will not be accused, reproached or criticized, but that everything will be judged as if through an open window. This always impresses people. If a couple have a quarrel and some one opens a window, the quarrel stops, and it is a wholly different situation. When a window is open and they can be heard, people do not want to give expression to their mistaken character traits. This is one step forward, and this is made when children come to the clinic.

III

This is the case of an oldest child, thirteen and a half years old.

At the age of eleven he had an I. Q. of 140.
It might, therefore, be said that this is a bright child.

Since he entered the second term of high school he has made very little progress.
From experience we know that if a child be-

lieves he is bright, he very often expects everything without effort, and the consequence is that such children are very often brought to a stop. We find, for instance that these children in the period of adolescence feel they are much more grown up than they really are. They want to prove that they are not children any more. The more they attempt to express themselves, the more they meet the difficulties of real life. They then begin to doubt whether they are really as clever as they have hitherto regarded themselves. It is not advisable to tell a child he is bright or that he has an I. Q. of 140. Children should never know their I. Q. and neither should the parents. All this explains why such a bright child should fail later. It is a situation fraught with danger. A child who is very ambitious and who is not sure of having a success in the right way, will look for a wrong way in which to be successful. Some of these wrong ways are: to become neurotic, to commit suicide, to commit crimes, to become lazy or to waste time. There are a hundred varieties of alibis that children use in order to be successful in a useless way.

Favorite subject is science. Associates with boys younger than himself.

We know that children join with younger children in order to have things easier; in order to be superior and be the leader. It is a suspicious sign if children like to associate with younger children, although it need not always be so—sometimes the attitude is that of a father. But there is always a certain weakness involved, because the expression of a paternal instinct involves the exclusion of play with older children. This exclusion is a conscious act.

Likes football and baseball.

We can presuppose, therefore, that he is very good in these games. Probably we shall hear that he is quite good in certain directions, but in some things not even interested. It means that wherever he is sure of success, there he will be active; wherever he is not sure of success, he refuses to participate. This is of course not the right way to act.

Plays cards.
That means wasting time.

This seems to take his attention away from the usual routine of going to bed early and doing his home work in the proper time.

Now we are coming to real complaints and these are all focused on the same point. He cannot go ahead in his studies and he therefore simply wastes time.

As an infant he developed slowly. After two years he began to develop rapidly.

In these two years we do not know why he developed slowly. He was probably pampered and what we have is the result of a pampered childhood. The slow development might have been due to this pampering. We see pampered children who do not want to speak or move or function because they like being supported, and they are thus not stimulated to develop. But when he develops rapidly the only explanation is that there was a stimulus for development. Probably there was some strong stimulus that made him a bright and intelligent child.

Outstanding features are honesty and stubbornness.

It is not enough for us that he is honest. It is all very nice and is really an advantage, but we do not know if he does not use this honesty in order to criticize others. It may very well be a way for him to boast. We know that he is a person who likes to lead and to boss others, and this honesty could be an expression of his superiority striving. We are not sure whether if this boy were in an unfavorable situation he could continue to be honest. As regards his stubbornness, we find that he really wants his own way and likes to be different and not led by others.

He bullies his younger brother.

In this statement our judgment is confirmed. He wants to be a leader, and because his younger brother does not obey he bullies him. This is not very honest and you will find, if you really know him, that he is something of a liar. He is a boasting person and we see his feeling of superiority. What is expressed here is really a superiority complex, but this superiority complex shows clearly that he is at bottom suffering from a sense of inferiority. He undervalues himself because overvalued by others, and because he undervalues himself, he has to make up for it by boasting. It is not wise to praise a child too much because then he gets the idea that much is expected of him. When he does not find it easy to meet expectations, he begins to tremble and to be afraid, and the result is that he will organize his life so that his weakness will not be discovered. Ergo, he bullies his brother, etc. This is his style of life. He does not feel strong enough and confident enough to solve the problems of life independently and properly. Hence his passion for playing cards. When he plays cards nobody can discover his inferiority, even if he has bad school reports. The parents would say his bad reports are due to the fact that he always plays cards, and in this way his pride and vanity are saved. He becomes imbued with this idea: "Yes, because I like cards I am not a good pupil; if I did not play cards I would be the best pupil. But, I play cards." He is satisfied, and he has the comfortable feeling that he *could* be the best. As long as this boy does not understand the logic of his own psychology he can wail to himself and hide his feeling of inferiority both from himself and from others. And so long as he can do this, he will not change. Hence, in a very friendly manner, we must reveal to him the springs of his character and show him that he really acts like a person who does not feel strong enough to accomplish his work. He feels strong enough only to hide his feeling of weakness, his feeling of inferiority. This should be done as we have said, in a friendly manner and with constant encouragement. We should not always praise him and wave his high I. Q. before him—this constant reminder was probably what made him afraid he might not always have success. We know quite well that later in life the I. Q. is not very important; all good experimental psychologists know that an I. Q. can only show a present situation as revealed in the test and that life is too complicated and cannot be known in a test. A high I. Q. is no proof that a child is really able to solve all the problems of life.

The boy's real difficulty is his lack of social-mindedness and his feeling of inferiority. And this must be explained to him.

IV

This is the case of a boy eight and a half years old. This case illustrates how children are pampered. Criminal and neurotic types spring chiefly from the class of pampered children. The great need of our age is that we stop pampering children. This does not mean that we have to stop liking them, but it means that we have to stop indulging them. We should treat them like friends and equals. This case is valuable for the way it portrays the features of a pampered child.

THE EDUCATION OF CHILDREN

Present problem: Repeated every grade in school and is now only in the 2A grade.

A child who repeats classes in the first years of school may very well be suspected of feeble-mindedness. We must keep that possibility in mind in our analysis. On the other hand, with a child who starts out well and then slumps, feeble-mindedness may be ruled out.

Talks baby talk.

He wants to be pampered: therefore he imitates a baby. But this means that he must have a purpose and goal in mind, since he regards it as an advantage to act like a baby. The existence of a rational conscious plan in this case rules out feeble-mindedness. He did not like school work as he was not prepared for school. And so, instead of developing along social lines in school, he expresses his striving by antagonizing and fighting the environment. This attitude of antagonism is of course paid for by his being left back in every class.

Disobeys and fights badly with the older brother.

Hence we see that the older brother is for him a hindrance. From this we can presuppose that the older brother must be a good pupil. The only way he can compete with his older brother is by being bad. Also in his dream life he imagines he would be ahead of his brother if he were a baby.

Walked at twenty-two months.
He probably suffered from rickets. If he did not walk until twenty-two months then it is also probable that he was always watched, and that his mother was with him continually during these twenty-two months. We can see how this organic imperfection has been a stimulus for the mother to watch him more and pamper him.

He talked early.
Now we are sure that he is not feeble-minded. Feeble-mindedness is expressed largely in the difficulty of learning to speak.

He always talks baby talk. The father is very affectionate.
He also pampers him.

He prefers the mother. There are two boys in the family. Mother says the older boy is clever. The two boys fight a great deal.
It is a case of rivalry of children in the family.

It is present in most families, especially between the first two children in the family, but there is often rivalry between any two children who grow up together. The psychology of the situation is the fact that when another child comes along, the first is dethroned, and, as we have seen (Chap. 8) the situation can be prevented only if children are properly prepared for co-operation.

He does poorly in arithmetic.
The greatest difficulty in school for the pampered child is usually arithmetic, for arithmetic involves a certain social logic which pampered children do not have.

There must be something wrong with his head.
We cannot find it. He acts quite intelligently.

The mother and teacher believe that he masturbates.
It is possible that he does. Most children do masturbate.

The mother says he has dark rings under his eyes.
We cannot properly conclude to the practice of

masturbation from the presence of rings under the eyes, although people generally are suspicious of it.

He is very finicky in eating.
We see how he always wants to occupy his mother, even in connection with his eating.

He is afraid of the dark.
Being afraid of the dark is also a sign of a pampered childhood.

The child's mother says he has a lot of friends.
We believe they are the ones he can boss.

He is interested in music.
It is instructive to examine the external ear among musical persons. One finds that the ear of a musical person has better developed curves. When we saw this boy we were positive that he had a fine and sensitive ear. This sensitiveness may express itself in a liking for harmony, and the person that possesses it may have a greater capacity for musical training.

He likes to sing, but he has ear trouble.
Such persons cannot easily endure our noisy life. Among such persons the tendency to ear infections

is greater than among others. The formation of the auditory organ is inherited, and that is why both musical talent and ear trouble are passed on from generation to generation. This boy is suffering from ear trouble and in his family are some very musical persons.

The proper course of treatment for the boy is to try to make him more independent and self-reliant. At present he is not self-reliant, but believes that it is necessary for his mother always to occupy herself with him and never to leave him alone. He is always wanting to be supported by the mother, and mothers are of course only too glad to give this support. He is now to be free to do what he wants —free to make mistakes. For it is only in this way that he can learn self-reliance. He is to learn not to compete with his brother for his mother's favor. At present each brother feels that the other is preferred, and each one is therefore needlessly jealous of the other.

What is especially necessary is to make the boy courageous enough to face the problems of school life. For, think what will happen if he does not continue at school. The moment he breaks with school he will have deviated to the useless side of life. One day he will play hookey from school, another day he will stop school altogether, disappear from home and join a gang. An ounce of prevention is worth a pound of cure; it is better to adjust him now to school life than to have to deal later with a juvenile delinquent. The school is now the crucial test. At present he is not prepared to solve problems in a social way and that is why he has difficulties at school. But it is up to the school to give him new courage. Of course the school has its own problems: perhaps the classes are overcrowded, and perhaps the teachers that he has come across are not well prepared for this work of psychological encouragement. That is the tragedy of things. But if this boy can find a single teacher who can encourage and hearten him properly, then he will be saved.

v

A case history of a girl ten years of age.

Referred to the clinic from school because of difficulties with arithmetic and spelling.
Arithmetic is usually a difficult subject for a pampered child. There is no rule that pampered children must be bad pupils in arithmetic, but we have very often found this to be our experience.

300

We know that very often left-handed children have difficulties in spelling because they are trained to look from the right to the left side and when they read they read from the right to the left. They read and spell correctly, but reverse. Usually nobody understands that they read in the right way, only reverse. They know only that they cannot read and they will simply say that they cannot read or spell correctly. Thus we suspect that the girl may be left-handed. Perhaps there is another reason why she has difficulties in spelling. In New York we must think of the possibility that perhaps she is from another country, and therefore does not understand English properly. In Europe we do not have to take such a thought into account.

Important points in past history: The family lost most of its money in Germany.

We do not know when they came from Germany. This girl probably had once experienced good times which suddenly came to an end. This is always a new situation which is like a test. In this new situation it will be revealed whether she has been rightly trained for co-operation and whether she is socially adjusted and courageous. It will also be revealed whether or not she can bear the burden of being poor—which means in other words, whether she can co-operate. It seems that she cannot co-operate properly.

She was a good pupil in Germany, and was eight years old when she left Germany.

This was two years ago.

She does not get along well in school here because the spelling is difficult and arithmetic is not taught in the same way as in Germany.

The teacher does not always make allowances for this.

Pampered by the mother, to whom she is very much attached. Likes both parents the same.

If you ask children the question "Whom do you prefer, your mother or your father?" they will generally give the answer, "I like them both the same!" They are taught to give this answer to such a question. There are many ways to test the truth of this answer. A good way is to put the child between the two parents and when we speak to the parents the child will move towards the one to whom she is most attached. We can see the same thing when the parents are in a room and the child enters. Again she will go to the one to whom she is most attached.

She has a few girl friends of her own age, but not many. Earliest remembrances: At the age of eight she was in the country with her parents and used to play with a dog in the grass. They also had a carriage at this time.

She remembers her riches, the grass, the dog and the carriage. It is the same as with a man who was formerly rich and always looks back to the days when he had a car, horses, a fine house, servants, etc. We can understand that she does not feel contented.

Dreams about Christmas and what Santa Claus will bring her.

Her dream life expresses the same outlook as her waking life. She always wants to have more because she feels deprived and wants to regain what she has had in the past.

Leans on the mother.

This is a sign of her discouragement and of her difficulties at school. It was explained to her that things were harder for her than for the other children and that she could learn by studying more and by being courageous.

She came to the clinic again, without her mother. She is getting along a little better in school and has been doing everything alone at home.

She was advised to be independent, not to depend upon the mother and do everything alone.

She cooked breakfast for father.

This is a sign of a sense of developing co-operation.

She believes she is more courageous, and seemed to be more at ease in this interview.

She is to return and bring the mother.

She returned with the mother, who came for the first time. The mother had been working hard and could not get away before. She reports that the child is a foster child and was adopted when two years old, and does not know that she is a foster child. In her first two years she was in six different places.

This is not a nice past. It seems as though this girl suffered very much in the first two years. Thus we have to do with a child who was probably once hated and neglected and then came into the good care of this woman. The child wants to cling to this favorable situation because of the unconscious impression in her mind of her early bad experiences. In two years a child can be very much impressed.

When the mother took the child she was told that she must be very strict as the child's family was not a good one.

The person who gave this advice was poisoned with the idea of heredity. If she should be strict and the girl should turn out a problem child then the judge would say, "You see, I am right!" He would not know that he is the guilty one.

The mother was bad and the foster mother feels a greater responsibility for the girl because she is not her own child. She sometimes hits the child.

The situation is not so favorable as before. The pampering attitude ceases sometimes and instead she is punished.

The father pampers the child and gives her whatever she wants. If she wants something she will not say "please" or "thank you." She says "you are not my mother."

Either the child knows the fact or uses a phrase which hits the right spot. We know of a boy of twenty, who does not believe his mother is his real mother, and yet the parents swear that the child could not know it. Evidently he had such a feeling. Children form conclusions out of very small things. "The child does not know she is adopted," but sometimes they feel it.

She says this to the mother but not to the father. The father does not give her a chance to attack him in that way because he gives her everything.

The mother cannot understand the change at the new school. Now she has a bad report card and she has had to hit her. The poor child has a bad report card, she is humiliated and feels inferior, and then the mother spanks her—it is too much. Even one of these two things would be too much—either to be spanked or to get a bad school report. This is a matter to be considered by the teachers, who should realize that when they give children bad school reports, it is the beginning of more trouble at home. A wise teacher would avoid giving bad school reports if she knew that the bad reports would be an occasion for the mother to spank the child.

The child says that she sometimes forgets herself and has an outburst of temper. She is excited at school and corrupts the class. She believes she must always be the first.

We can understand this desire in an only child trained by the father to get everything that she wants. We can understand that she likes to be the first. We know that in the past she had the country fields, etc., and that she feels deprived of her past advantages. Now her superiority striving is much stronger, but as she has no channels for its expression, she forgets herself and makes trouble.

It was explained to her that she must learn to co-operate. We told her that she gets excited in order to be the center of attention, and that her outbursts of temper are only an excuse to get everybody to look at her. She does not work in school because her mother is angry with her reports and she is fighting the mother.

Dreams that Santa Claus brought her many things. Then she awakes and finds nothing.

Here again she wants always to arouse such feelings and emotions of having everything that she wants and "awakes and finds nothing." We must not overlook the snake in the grass. If we arouse such feelings and emotions in a dream and awake and see nothing, then we will naturally feel

307

disappointed. Yet the dream arouses only the feelings which are consistent with the attitude after awakening. In other words, the emotional goal of the dreams is not the arousing of marvelous feelings of possessing everything—the emotional goal is precisely, to be disappointed. It is for this purpose that the dreams are created until the goal is satisfied and the disappointment takes place. In melancholia, persons have marvelous dreams but awake and find things quite the contrary. We can understand why this girl wants to be disappointed. She wants to accuse the mother since her present life must appear to her in very dark colors. She feels that she has nothing and the mother does not give her anything. "She spanks me; only father gives me things."

Summing up this case we can see that the child always wants to be disappointed so that she can accuse the mother. She is fighting the mother and if we want to stop this fight, we must be able to convince her that her behavior at home, her dreams and her behavior at school are all of the same mistaken pattern. Her mistaken style of life is largely the result of the fact that she has been only a short time in America, and is not very well trained in the English language. We must therefore convince her that these difficulties could be easily overcome, but that she is deliberately using them as a weapon with which to fight her mother. We must also influence the mother to stop spanking the child, so as not to give her an excuse for fighting. The child must be brought to realize that "I am not attentive and forget myself, and have outbursts of temper because I want to have trouble with my mother." If she knows this, then she can stop her bad behavior. Before she knew the meaning of all the experiences and impressions in her home and school life and in her dreams, a change of character was of course out of the question.

And so we see what Psychology is—to understand the use a person makes of his impressions and experiences. Or, in other words, Psychology means to understand the scheme of apperception by which the child acts and by which he reacts to stimuli, to understand how he regards certain stimuli, how he responds to them, and how he uses them for his own purposes.